TO THE ENDS OF THE EARTH

ACTION

TO THE ENDS
OF THE EARTH
ACTION

MARK C. MCCANN

Our Sunday Visitor

www.osv.com
Our Sunday Visitor Publishing Division
Our Sunday Visitor, Inc.
Huntington, Indiana 46750

Our Sunday Visitor Publishing Division
Our Sunday Visitor, Inc.
200 Noll Plaza
Huntington, IN 46750
1-800-348-2440

ISBN: 978-1-68192-384-0 (Inventory No. T2267)
eISBN: 978-1-68192-385-7
LCCN: 2018959071

Cover design: Tyler Ottinger
Cover art: Shutterstock.com
Interior design: Lindsey Riesen

PRINTED IN THE UNITED STATES OF AMERICA

To my father-in-law, Gerald Davino, who taught me that a Catholic man is both a strong leader and a solid friend, a tireless and tender provider for his family, and a serious and sober defender of the Faith. You are a true follower of Christ — a believer with an open heart, a humble worldview, and a willingness to grow as a man of God. Thank you for being a shining example of Christian manhood and for accepting me into your family. Thank you most of all for nurturing the daughter who became my beautiful bride and shared God's salvation story with me.

TABLE OF CONTENTS

PREFACE

We are on the path to perfection. Who we are in Christ forms the foundation for right living and sets us on the path toward a glorious eternity in the presence of our heavenly Father. If we want to reach our destination, each of us must make a commitment. We must put on the virtues God has given to us in Christ.

Are we strong in our faith, standing on the rock-solid foundation of the Word and the Church, or are we double-minded men, tossed to and fro on the waves of our own indecisiveness (cf. Eph 4:14)? Are we troubled by a painful past, locked in a prison of sin from which we cannot break free, or do we listen to the still, small voice of the One who breaks our bonds and sets our feet on the right path? We must turn our worlds upside down, being willing to lose in order to gain. We must strive with single-minded purpose to win, empowered by God alone, forgetting our past and allowing him to change us radically into the men he created us to be.

During the next ten weeks, we will be looking at the simple truths of our faith — the no-nonsense, straightforward gospel message that shows us how we should act if we want to stay on the straight and narrow path toward heaven. Throughout this study, we will focus on the virtues we need to be strong men of God. At the same time, we will be growing in fellowship with our brothers and fixing our eyes on Jesus, the author and finisher of our faith (cf. Heb 12:2).

As you pore over the selected passages from Scripture throughout this study, remember that all of our actions should be rooted in love. Love is the glue that holds all other virtues together; the beautiful gift that completes our faith and moves us along the path of salvation (cf. Col 3:14). Be sure to spend quality time with other men, sharing openly about what it means to be given a second chance in Christ, to carry through our trials in his strength, and to love others as he has loved us.

This book is both a personal daily devotional and a tool for group study with other men. Each day, you are encouraged to read through the day's devotion, pray and meditate on the message from God's Word, and reflect on the questions provided, always remembering the theme for the week and seeking to apply it to your life. It is suggested that you take fifteen to thirty minutes in the morning to complete each devotion, and then let your prayerful experience with the Lord guide you throughout your day.

On Saturday you are encouraged to look back on your week of study, reflecting on the progress you've made, thanking God for the work he has done in your life, throwing any mistakes into the ocean of God's mercy, and committing to personal goals in areas where you'd like to see improvement in the coming week.

Those who want to take things a step further are encouraged to keep a journal where you write your reflections, track your progress in Christian living, and dialogue with the God who is leading you on this journey of manhood. You can then use your journal to help you share your insights and discoveries with other men.

The key to growing with this study involves two things: taking time to read and learn each day, and then living out the message through practical acts of love. This means taking the reflection questions and turning them into action steps that you can do as you love your family, serve your church and community, and lift up your brothers in the Faith.

Once a week you are encouraged to come together with

other Catholic men to share your thoughts on the devotions, the insights you have gained in prayer, and the ways you have put these principles into practice in everyday life. The leader of your study group will facilitate a discussion, focusing on those passages, reflections, and actions that have meant the most to the men in the group. After a general sharing of thoughts about the daily devotions, the leader can focus on the Saturday "Go Deeper" questions. As each man shares ideas, the leader will encourage the other men to build on the ideas raised and add their own unique voices to the discussion.

As you make this journey, determine to spend more time in prayer, study, and worship to grow in your faith. Look for opportunities to interact with your brothers as you build one another up, carry one another's burdens, and hold one another accountable before God. Love your families and your communities with the same uncompromising love that Christ has poured out on you. Look for ways to make this world a better place by being a man who represents Christ and his Church well. And look forward to all the blessings that are to come in God's good time!

INTRODUCTION

CHARACTER LIVED OUT WITHIN THE WORLD

Being a man of action is something that flows from your godly character. Hopefully you have examined your inner man by completing Book I of the *To the Ends of the Earth* series, *Character*. Now it's time to put that knowledge into practice by considering how to will and to act according to the will of God. We need to be men who draw our strength from the table of the Lord, who seek the nourishment of the Word and the Eucharist, who unburden ourselves in the confessional and march boldly into the arena of life carrying the truth of the gospel.

In order to act on God's behalf, we need to yield our self-centered ways to the sacrificial love of Christ. It is his voice alone that we must follow. That voice speaks to us in subtle ways, leading us to daily victories, great and small. It helps us to band together with our Catholic brothers and to act according to the great paradox of Christianity: to lose everything we hold dear to gain eternity in heaven. Every word we speak and every deed we do will leave a lasting legacy upon this earth. As Catholic men of action, we must draw our strength from the God who forgives our faults and draws us ever homeward, one faithful step at a time.

I invite you to read this study and to activate it daily by all you say and do. Be a loud, proud, bold Catholic man, unashamed of his faith, and always ready to build the kingdom, to raise up your brothers and to live sold-out lives for the glory of God!

WEEK 1

TABLE MANNERS

*Whoever, therefore, eats the bread or drinks the cup of the Lord
in an unworthy manner will be guilty of profaning the body
and blood of the Lord. Let a man examine himself, and so eat
of the bread and drink of the cup. For any one who eats and
drinks without discerning the body eats and drinks judgment
upon himself.*

1 Corinthians 11:27–29

The Eucharist is central to our lives as Catholics. It is not
simply a representation of the Last Supper; it is, as Pope
Francis has said, the Last Supper itself. When we attend Mass,
we literally experience the Passion and redeeming death of the
Lord.[1] As Jesus himself said, the Eucharist is "true food" and
"true drink" (Jn 6:55). We have been given a great gift in the
Eucharist. It satisfies our deepest desire for peace, feeds our
most profound hunger for purpose, and stirs us to great joy.

Do we understand what we receive in Communion, Sunday after Sunday? Do we recognize the Body and the Blood of

---

1. Pope Francis, Morning Meditation in the Chapel of the *Domus Sanctae Marthae*, "At
Mass without a Watch," February 10, 2014, https://w2.vatican.va/content/francesco/
en/cotidie/2014/documents/papa-francesco-cotidie_20140210_mass-without-watch.
html.

the Lord as we receive the Eucharist? Do we come with clean hearts and open hands, ready to participate fully in the Sacrifice of the Mass and to be sent out into the world to spread the Good News of Jesus by our words and deeds? Or do we come with broken spirits, hardened hearts, and closed minds, unable to set aside our selfishness and take on the task of spreading the gospel? As Catholic men, we must be willing to give ourselves over to our Savior, allowing him to lead us to the table of his Body and Blood with resolve and understanding.

In our call to follow Christ, to take up our crosses and walk the walk of self-surrender, we must become like Christ. That means we are to be broken bread and poured out wine for the world. The Eucharist gives us the strength to be men after God's own heart, to sacrifice ourselves in the service of the gospel for our families, our Church, and our world. The beauty, power, and presence of the Eucharist are absolutely foundational to our lives and actions as Catholic men. In fact, all of our actions should flow from our encounter with the Eucharistic Lord.

How do we allow the Eucharist to transform our every action? The sixth chapter of the ospel of John has the answers. This week we will focus on five key points from this important gospel:

1. The Eucharist gives life.
Jesus says that he is the true bread that comes down from heaven to give life to the world (cf. Jn 6:32–35). His sacrificial death on the cross provides our salvation, and we relive that saving act every time we receive the Body and Blood of the Lord.

2. The Eucharist is about abundance.
The Bread of Life Discourse in John 6 takes place after Jesus feeds the 5,000. The people wanted the miracle of the loaves to continue. Jesus offered them a much greater abundance — he promised eternal life in him.

3. The Eucharist is about satisfaction.

Those who partake of the Body and Blood of Christ will never hunger or thirst again (cf. Jn 6:35, 58). Even more importantly, in the Eucharist we know that Christ has made complete satisfaction for our sins. There is no further need for sacrifices because the once-for-all sacrifice of Christ on the cross is complete satisfaction for humanity's sins, and we are allowed to partake in that sacrifice whenever we receive the Eucharist.

4. The Eucharist is about making an eternal decision.

We are asked to give our "Amen!" when we receive the Eucharist. Part of this assent is accepting Christ's offer of salvation through his death on the cross. We can say yes to his call, or we can murmur in disbelief like those who rejected the truth of the Eucharist as a "hard" saying.

5. The Eucharist is about love.

Jesus knew that many would reject him because of the Eucharist, but still he offered his love to the world. Like Peter, each of us can return that love by acknowledging that only Jesus has the words of everlasting life and by giving our lives fully to him.

This Week's Call to Action

As Catholic men, we must stand firm in our faith in the Eucharist so that we can bring the presence of Christ to a hurting world. Past, present, and future come together in every celebration of the Mass, as the priest speaks the words of Consecration over the bread and wine. This is a moment so profound that our only response should be one of thanksgiving and awe. The bread of the earth and the fruit of the vine become the very Body, Blood, Soul, and Divinity of Christ!

This means that the way in which we partake of the Eucharist is very important. We cannot become witnesses to the world if we sin against the Body and Blood of the Lord through hearts hardened by selfishness and sin. As we receive, so we are sent out into the world, to be broken bread and poured out wine for all those who hunger and thirst for Jesus.

This week consider how you will live out this incredible truth. Allow Christ to transform all of your actions through the power of the Eucharist, so that you can be a true servant of the kingdom. As you interact with others, particularly other men, find ways to share the life, abundance, satisfaction, commitment, and love of the Eucharist in all you say and do. Speak truth into other men's lives. Give generously of your time and talent to meet their needs. Commit to praying for and supporting these men throughout this study and beyond. Share with them the sacrificial and life-changing love of Jesus Christ.

SUNDAY

This week we will meditate on the power of the Eucharist. We will consider the reality of the Body and Blood of the Lord as expressed in the Gospels. We will ponder the abundant and satisfying grace that is ours through this Sacrament. We will strive to live in full awareness that each time we receive the Eucharist, we are experiencing the supreme sacrifice Christ made on the cross to take away our sins. Hopefully we will experience the great love Christ pours out for each of us in this Sacrament and look for practical ways to share that love with others.

As you join with your brothers and sisters at Mass this Sunday, be mindful of the words of Jesus from John 6. Meditate on the rejection he faced as he spoke about people eating his Body and drinking his Blood. Listen to the words of Peter, as he tells the Lord that there is no other to whom we can turn, for Jesus alone has the words of eternal life. Consider how Jesus left us this great sign as the center of our worship. The Eucharist truly takes us to the moment when heaven and earth were reconciled in the greatest act of love: Christ's saving death on the cross.

Pray a prayer of thanksgiving to Christ. If you are able to meet with other men this week, share your reflections and any insights that may have come to you during Mass.

Questions for reflection

How can I develop a greater love for the Eucharist?

Do I approach Communion in a worthy manner, receiving the Body and Blood of the Lord with joy and thanksgiving?

How is Jesus asking me to take him out to the lost and hurting of this world?

Praying with Scripture

"And he took bread, and when he had given thanks he broke it and gave it to them, saying, 'This is my body which is given for you. Do this in remembrance of me.' And likewise the chalice after supper, saying, 'This chalice which is poured out for you is the new covenant in my blood'" (Lk 22:19–20).

MONDAY
THE EUCHARIST GIVES LIFE

"I am the living bread which came down from heaven; if any one eats of this bread, he will live for ever; and the bread which I shall give for the life of the world is my flesh." The Jews then disputed among themselves, saying, "How can this man give us his flesh to eat?" So Jesus said to them, "Truly, truly, I say to you, unless you eat the flesh of the Son of man and drink his blood, you have no life in you; he who eats my flesh and drinks my blood has eternal life, and I will raise him up at the last day."

John 6:51–54

Jesus came to bring us life — his life. Nothing else can satisfy our hunger for meaning and peace. Nothing else can bring us salvation. The Eucharist is the true bread that came down from heaven, the Body, Blood, Soul, and Divinity of our Savior. When Jesus left us this sacrament, he left us a share in his very life, for his Body and Blood are real food and drink. When we partake of the Eucharist, we are not simply remembering Christ's sacrifice on Calvary; we are truly there at the foot of the cross.

This is not merely a symbol or a nice idea, but a deep reality, even though it is so far beyond what our senses can grasp. This living sign has been given to us to strengthen us and draw us into the very act of our salvation. It gives us all the graces we need to live out our salvation in every act of love we share, at every moment of our lives — all for the glory of God.

It should be noted that Christ's discourse on the Eucharist is the only incident recorded in the Gospels where people turned away from Jesus for doctrinal reasons. They rejected Our Lord's words because they were too difficult for their hardened hearts to bear. Our call as Catholic men is to accept the powerful truth of the Eucharist and to carry that truth to the world. Humanity is hungering for the life that only Jesus can bring through his death on the cross. We must be willing to share that same life that we have received at Baptism and continue to experience in the Eucharist.

Questions for Reflection

What does it mean to you to be able to receive the Eucharist each Sunday?

How does participating in the Sacrifice of the Mass strengthen you to act in a godly way?

How will you share the life of Christ given to you in the Eucharist with other men this week?

Praying with Scripture

"Jesus said to them, 'I am the bread of life; he who comes to me shall not hunger, and he who believes in me shall never thirst'" (Jn 6:35).

TUESDAY
THE EUCHARIST IS ABOUT ABUNDANCE

Ho, every one who thirsts,
*   come to the waters;*
and he who has no money,
*   come, buy and eat!*
Come, buy wine and milk
*   without money and without price.*
Why do you spend your money for that which is not bread,
*   and your labor for that which does not satisfy?*
Listen diligently to me, and eat what is good,
*   and delight yourselves in rich food.*
Incline your ear, and come to me;
*   hear, that your soul may live;*
and I will make with you an everlasting covenant,
*   my steadfast, merciful love for David.*
Behold, I made him a witness to the peoples,
*   a leader and commander for the peoples.*
Behold, you shall call nations that you know not,
*   and nations that knew you not shall run to you,*
because of the LORD your God, and of the Holy One of Israel,
*   for he has glorified you.*

Isaiah 55:1–5

Jesus miraculously fed a crowd of 5,000 men, not including women and children. This happened just before his Bread of Life Discourse. He had provided an abundant banquet for those who had spent the day listening to his teachings. They came hungering for something to fill the longing in their hearts and the emptiness in their lives. Jesus could not send them away without satisfying their needs.

His actions prefigured the Sacrifice of the Mass. He gathered the people, called them to a time of worship, preached the Word, proclaimed the Good News, and shared a sacred, miraculous meal before sending the people forth in love. What an abundant gift!

The glory of the Eucharist is that it is far more than we could ever have hoped for or imagined. It is the most abundant blessing from God, the sign of his great sacrifice on Calvary, the Supper of the Lamb, who gave his life for the world. It nourishes our weary souls and fills us to overflowing so that we can spill over with love for the world that Christ is calling home to himself. The people came to Jesus seeking perishable food; Jesus offered them abundant, eternal life.

We are called to the fullness of Eucharistic life in all our actions. As we participate in the Eucharist, we are strengthened to offer the same abundant blessing we have received from Christ to all those who are looking for what will satisfy their souls.

Questions for Reflection

Do you recognize the Eucharist as a gift that flows from God's abundance? If not, what keeps you from seeing it in that way?

What are some other abundant blessings God has given to you?

Who in your life needs the life-giving power of the Eucharist? How can you help bring them to it?

Praying with Scripture

"And God is able to provide you with every blessing in abundance, so that you may always have enough of everything and may provide in abundance for every good work. As it is written, 'He scatters abroad, he gives to the poor; his righteousness endures for ever'" (2 Cor 9:8–9).

WEDNESDAY
THE EUCHARIST IS ABOUT SATISFACTION

Consequently he is able for all time to save those who draw near to God through him, since he always lives to make intercession for them. For it was fitting that we should have such a high priest, holy, blameless, unstained, separated from sinners, exalted above the heavens. He has no need, like those high priests, to offer sacrifices daily, first for his own sins and then for those of the people; he did this once for all when he offered up himself. Indeed, the law appoints men in their weakness as high priests, but the word of the oath, which came later than the law, appoints a Son who has been made perfect for ever.

Hebrews 7:25–28

Not only is the Eucharist about the abundant love of Jesus Christ; it is also about perfect satisfaction. God in his justice demanded a perfect sacrifice to make up for our sins, and no human being could offer such a sacrifice. Only someone who was divine and human could make the needed reparation for our fallen nature. So God in his mercy sent his Son Jesus, true God and true man, to be our Great High Priest and our perfect sacrifice. Jesus, by living a sinless human life and offering up that life on the cross, satisfied the debt for our sins.

The priests of the Old Testament had to repeat their sacrifices year after year, and these sacrifices did not come close to making satisfaction for sin. Jesus needed to offer up his perfect sacrifice only one time. The Eucharist does not repeat the sacrifice of Christ. Instead, it is the once-for-all sacrifice of Calvary.

Moreover, the Eucharist fully satisfies our deepest hunger. Our separation from God as a result of Adam's sin leaves us with an emptiness that only Christ can fill. Through his Body and Blood, Jesus provides us with real food and real drink. As we receive the Bread of Life and the Chalice of Eternal Salvation, we know we will never hunger or thirst again. Every longing, every need, and every desire finds its fulfillment in Christ's sacrifice on the cross.

Questions for Reflection

Do you recognize that Jesus has made satisfaction, not just for the sins of the world, but for your personal sins as well? How do you thank him for this gift?

Do you participate fully and with gratitude in the Sacrifice of the Mass? If not, what can you do to improve your attention?

How has the Eucharist satisfied some of your deepest longings?

Praying with Scripture

"I will abundantly bless [Zion's] provisions; / I will satisfy her poor with bread" (Ps 132:15).

THURSDAY
THE EUCHARIST IS ABOUT MAKING AN ETERNAL DECISION

"I call heaven and earth to witness against you this day, that I have set before you life and death, blessing and curse; therefore choose life, that you and your descendants may live, loving the LORD your God, obeying his voice, and clinging to him; for that means life to you and length of days, that you may dwell in the land which the LORD swore to your fathers, to Abraham, to Isaac, and to Jacob, to give them."

Deuteronomy 30:19–20

God's people were preparing to enter the promised land. Moses called each one to make an eternal decision: to choose life or death, heaven or hell, peace and prosperity or division and ruin. To choose life was to choose God and to receive his offer of a future salvation. His challenge to the people is our challenge every Sunday at Mass. The Eucharist is our ultimate life choice. To make such a choice lightly is to profane the Body and Blood of the Lord. Like the Israelites, we can either receive or reject the life that Christ offers us in the Eucharist.

Sadly, many Catholics go through the motions of the Mass, never fully realizing what the Eucharist is. Christians of many denominations talk about "making a decision" for Christ, but Catholics are given that opportunity every time we participate in the Mass. Our "Amen!" when we receive Communion is our "Yes!" to two things: (1) to the reality of Christ's True Presence in the Eucharist, and (2) to the salvation he won for us in his death on the cross, which is made present again in every Mass.

How we respond to the Eucharist truly matters. Saint Paul even talked about receiving the Eucharist in an unworthy manner: "For anyone who eats and drinks without discerning the body, eats and drinks judgment upon himself" (1 Cor 11:29). Our Catholic Faith is no simple matter. Each Sunday as we participate in the sacrifice of the Mass, we renew our commitment to follow Christ. Like the people in Moses' day, we are being offered a choice between life and death. Let us choose life and let us live that life to the fullest, by our prayers, our words, our actions, and all that we are!

Questions for reflection

Is there one thing you can do to improve your participation in the Mass? What is that one thing? Can you share it with a brother and ask him to hold you accountable to it?

When you say "Amen!" as you receive Communion, do you really think about what you are saying? Can you truly say that you mean it?

Praying with Scripture

"For all the promises of God find their Yes in him. That is why we utter the Amen through him, to the glory of God" (2 Cor 1:20).

FRIDAY
THE EUCHARIST IS ABOUT LOVE

Beloved, let us love one another; for love is of God, and he who loves is born of God and knows God. He who does not love does not know God; for God is love. In this the love of God was made manifest among us, that God sent his only-begotten Son into the world, so that we might live through him.

1 John 4:7–9

There are many kinds of love: romantic love, brotherly love, the love of beauty or art, etc. But there is one love that surpasses all others: *agape*, which is the love that is willing to surrender all things for the good of another.

That is what Jesus did. He gave his life for us to make us worthy to enter the kingdom of Heaven. Jesus knew that many would reject his teaching on the Eucharist, yet he did not hold back on speaking the truth about it. As a result, many of his followers walked away. When Jesus asked his disciples if they wished to leave him also, "Simon Peter answered him, 'Lord, to whom shall we go? You have the words of eternal life; and we have believed, and have come to know, that you are the Holy One of God'" (Jn 6:68–69).

We can take comfort in these words of Peter. Will we be like Peter and acknowledge that there is no other who can satisfy all our longings? Let us today commit our lives more fully to our Savior and carry out his call to share the gospel with the lost. Let us take in the words from John's Gospel and marvel at the love that made the Lord of the universe our friend. May we choose this day to love others as Jesus has loved us.

Questions for Reflection
How are you living out Christ's command to love others as he has loved you?

What one person in your life can you love in a sacrificial way today, following Jesus' example?

How can you help another man draw near to the One who has the words of eternal life?

Praying with Scripture
"By this we know love, that he laid down his life for us; and we ought to lay down our lives for the brethren" (1 Jn 3:16).

_____

SATURDAY

Go Deeper
How has Christ shown me his abundant life and love this week?

_____

_____

_____

_____

_____

_____

_____

Where do I find the most satisfaction in my faith? Why?

_____

_____

_____

_____

_____

Am I committed to loving and receiving Christ in the Eucharist? If not, what holds me back? What will I do to draw closer to him in the Blessed Sacrament?

_____

_____

_____

_____

_____

_____

Have I shown sacrificial love this week? If not, why not? If so, was I as generous as I could be?

_____

_____

_____

_____

_____

_____

_____

Do I show others the reality of the Eucharist in my words and deeds? Do I receive Communion with reverence? Do I let the Blessed Sacrament make a lasting impression on everything I say and do?

_____

_____

_____

_____

_____

WEEK 2

DOUBLE-MINDED OR FULLY JOYFUL

Count it all joy, my brethren, when you meet various trials, for you know that the testing of your faith produces steadfastness. And let steadfastness have its full effect, that you may be perfect and complete, lacking in nothing. If any of you lacks wisdom, let him ask God, who gives to all men generously and without reproaching, and it will be given him. But let him ask in faith, with no doubting, for he who doubts is like a wave of the sea that is driven and tossed by the wind. For that person must not suppose that a double-minded man, unstable in all his ways, will receive anything from the Lord.

James 1:2–8

Sin, while always connected to pride, is also a product of doubt. So often as Catholic men, we find ourselves facing trials and folding under pressure in our efforts to persevere. We find it difficult to consider it a joy that our faith is being tested. We hate weakness and failure, and trials bring us both. In the end, it is doubt that can cause us to stumble. When we are double-minded, unsure of our motives and our methods, unstable in all we say and do, we fall short of God's call to be men of action who build the kingdom on the sturdy foundation of Jesus Christ. When we doubt that God will supply the wisdom and the strength for us to see our trials through, we allow the enemy of our souls and this broken world to toss us about, leaving us floundering in our faith.

Saint James has the prescription for our doubting, double-minded, unstable ways. The whole first chapter of his letter offers the answers to finding the full measure of joy in the midst of trials:

1. We will boast in our lowly yet high standing.

James reminds us that a lowly man can "boast in his exultation" (Jas 1:9), because his source of strength comes from God alone. Accepting our lowliness helps to change our perspective and guides our actions. We recognize our need for God and become open to the transforming power of the trials of life that reshape us to serve the One who is our source of strength.

2. We must avoid the birth of sin.

James describes the power of temptation, which leads to the birth of sin if we give in to our own desires. Moreover, "sin when it is full-grown brings forth death" (v. 15). Temptation is the work of the world, the flesh, and the devil, not God. God gives us the power to persevere, not to fall, to discover our worth and purpose as we strive to avoid sin and to love as God has loved us.

3. We must not allow the sea of our troubles to toss us about.

We cannot receive God's wisdom and blessing if we are too busy being blown back and forth by our doubt (cf. v. 6). We must ask God to supply us with the assurance and understanding we need to navigate our struggles in faith so that we will be strong and steady men of action who build the kingdom by all we say and do.

4. We need to be men who act on the word we hear.

James compares those who hear the word and do nothing about it to a man looking at his reflection and then forgetting what he looks like (cf. v. 22–24). Faith without works is dead (cf. Jas 2:17). Acting on God's promises shows trust and fulfills the call to live out our faith through acts of charity.

5. We can look deeply into God's perfect law and be set free to love.

We need to focus all our spiritual attention on the depth of God's abiding love. As we gaze into the perfect Law of Love that sets us free, we find the strength to say no to sin and yes to all that God calls us to do for our world. We can grow stronger every day and become a blessing to others, sharing that perfect love that has so transformed us.

This Week's Call to Action

This week let love, service, and purity mark you as a joyful doer of the word. Accept that while trials are never pleasant, there is joy in trusting that God uses them to mold us into men who will not fold under pressure. Double-minded men make poor witnesses. When we accept our lowly position in God's plan and allow his wisdom to fuel our faith, we can become men of action who share our faith through our words and our deeds graced with the power of our Savior's perfect love.

See your struggles as a rigorous spiritual workout, letting God build your spiritual muscles as he shapes you into a man after his own heart. With each day that unfolds, accept the testing of your faith, knowing that God is making you stronger, destroying doubt, and teaching you how to love others and live with integrity. Remember that in Christ, believers become wise servants who stand strong against the waves of indecision and doubt. If we hold fast to faith, we can carry out his will with passion and power and a joy that is inexpressible.

SUNDAY

This week you will consider what it means to become singular-ly focused on the love of God as revealed in Jesus on the cross. You will work to avoid or overcome the birth of sin in your life. You will cast aside doubt and indecision and walk above the waves of adversity to rest on the shore of God's rock-solid care for you. You will strive to become a doer of the word and to work out your salvation with fear and trembling. You will be challenged to look boldly into the perfect Law of Love to discover the freedom to become the man God has made you to be. You will learn what it means to move from this stable place of faith and out into the world, where lost and hurting individuals are looking for that same love in their lives.

This Sunday, as you join in the celebration of the Eucharist, consider how God has lifted the veil and allowed you to enter into his heavenly realm. Meditate on the ways God has opened your eyes through the Church and her teachings. Think about your place in the Body of Christ, and reflect on God's call to be single-minded in your faith as you reach out to a weary world. As you receive the Body, Blood, Soul, and Divinity of Jesus Christ in the Eucharist, ask him to increase your faith and to set you free from any doubts that hold you back from living fully for him.

Dialogue with Jesus about his call in your life. Thank him for all he has done to bring you through your trials and strengthen you for your mission as a Catholic man.

Questions for Reflection

How can you develop a deeper trust in God so that his wisdom can give you stability and focus to carry out his will in your life?

Are there areas in your life where you are still double-minded, trying to walk in God's plan but conflicted by doubt? How can you surrender those areas to God this week?

What are some practical steps you can take this week to share the incredible reality of God's love with others?

Praying with Scripture
"Let us hold fast the confession of our hope without wavering, for he who promised is faithful" (Heb 10:23).

MONDAY
WE WILL BOAST IN OUR LOWLY YET HIGH STANDING

The LORD kills and brings to life;
    he brings down to Sheol and raises up.
The LORD makes poor and makes rich;
    he brings low, he also exalts.
He raises up the poor from the dust;
    he lifts the needy from the dung heap,
to make them sit with princes
    and inherit a seat of honor.
For the pillars of the earth are the LORD's,
    and on them he has set the world.

1 Samuel 2:6–8

The great paradox of the Christian life is that we achieve greatness in lowliness. To the worldly man, this is an insane contradiction. After all, why would anyone want to be lowly? But to Catholic men, this should be sensible and sound, because in Christ we are able to see with heaven's eyes. We understand that compared with God, all our efforts and our worth are filthy rags (cf. Is 64:6). The Good News, however, is that God takes our lowliness and raises it up. By his grace we are strengthened to live according to a higher calling. Our trials and our stumbling along the road of life allow God to refashion us in humility so we understand our true place in the universe. Though we are worth nothing, powerless and prideful, God lifts us from the dirt of this world and sets us up as princes among men.

We have become a new creation in Christ, and this shows us our purpose and our worth in God's eyes. He sees us through the saving work of Jesus on the cross. We become beautiful, worthy sons, who are called to rule our worlds with the same perfect love he has revealed to us. We recognize that every moment we experience — even our lowest — has a divine purpose in testing and shaping our souls. When we accept our trials and our lowliness, we become servants with hearts totally dedicated to the cause of Christ.

Questions for Reflection

Is it difficult for you to accept that only in lowliness you can become exalted? If so, why?

Where have you been striving to achieve greatness on your own merits?

How has God lifted you up in your lowliness? How has his saving work in your life given you a greater sense of your calling as a Catholic man?

Praying with Scripture

"He sets on high those who are lowly, and those who mourn are lifted to safety" (Jb 5:11).

TUESDAY
WE MUST AVOID THE BIRTH OF SIN

You meet him that joyfully works righteousness,
those that remember you in your ways.
Behold, you were angry, and we sinned;
in our sins we have been a long time, and shall

we be saved?
We have all become like one who is unclean,
   and all our righteous deeds are like a polluted garment.
We all fade like a leaf,
   and our iniquities, like the wind, take us away.
There is no one that calls upon your name,
   that bestirs himself to take hold of you.

Isaiah 64:5–7

Sin is a slippery slope that leads into a pit of destruction. It is a choice we make each and every time. It is not a work of God but part of our fallen nature. Once our desire surrenders to evil, we give birth to sin our lives, and if we allow it to linger, it will destroy us.

Proverbs 7 speaks of the seduction of a senseless and foolish man by an adulterous woman. The passage goes into great detail about the man's steady journey into sin. He makes his way secretly to her house, hears her seductive words, is enticed by what his senses take in, and then gives in to the sin of adultery. He is compared to an animal stepping into a snare and being captured, never to recover. This describes how sin works in our lives. It presents itself as a pleasurable experience, slowly drawing us into the trap it sets for us. We think it is something good, yet if we give ourselves over to it, ultimately it destroys our lives until our bodies, our minds, and our souls are left in utter turmoil.

We must remember that the temptation to sin does not come from God (cf. Jas 1:13), but from the world, the flesh, or the devil. When we give in to temptation, we have only our weak, sinful nature to blame. Yet when we repent, God takes the pain and devastation of sin and, through grace, transforms us and helps us persevere to the end. Let us remember that we are fallen men, incapable of accomplishing anything good outside of Christ. And let us thank God that in Christ we are set free to overcome sin and become men of integrity and purpose once more.

Questions for Reflection

What are some of your biggest struggles with temptation?

Do you ever blame God when you fall into sin? Why? What do you need to do to accept your own blame and surrender yourself to God's mercy?

How has God used the graces of the Sacrament of Confession to transform you?

How have your brothers in the Faith helped you to let go of sin and rely on grace?

Praying with Scripture

"Among these we all once lived in the passions of our flesh, following the desires of body and mind, and so we were by nature children of wrath, like the rest of mankind" (Eph 2:3).

WEDNESDAY
WE MUST NOT ALLOW THE SEA OF OUR TROUBLES TO TOSS US ABOUT

And behold, there arose a great storm on the sea, so that the boat was being swamped by the waves; but he was asleep. And they went and woke him, saying, "Save us, Lord; we are perishing." And he said to them, "Why are you afraid, O men of little faith?" Then he rose and rebuked the winds and the sea; and there was a great calm. And the men marveled, saying, "What sort of man is this, that even winds and sea obey him?"

Matthew 8:24–28

It can be tempting to believe that we can be good Christians without the Church. Especially in our society today, many men believe they can pray on their own, worship in their own way, and guide their own lives. They see the Church as unnecessary or even burdensome. But the truth is, without the Church we don't really have Christ in our lives, because the Church is his Body.

More than that, we need the Church to guide us, the ministry of her leaders to train us in the Faith, and the fellowship of her members to uplift and support us. The inevitable result of isolated Christianity is double-mindedness, hypocrisy, and vulnerability to falsehood and personal sin. Only in the Church can we reach out fully to Christ when waves of doubt and indecision threaten to overwhelm us.

Doubt can often do more damage than pride. It can keep us inactive in our faith or move us in directions contrary to God's will for our lives. As we are tossed back and forth by our fear and indecision, focused on the size of the storms we experience, we lose sight of the light of God's grace, which guides us to the safe shore of his love. God will give generously to those who come to him looking for the stability he offers in Christ. As we live out the Lord's command to love, we grow into rock-solid men able to bring change to our world.

Questions for Reflection
What does being double-minded look like in your life?

Where does it hold you back from trusting in Christ?

Where does doubt assail you? How can you invite Christ to calm the waves?

Do you have a strong relationship with the Church and your Catholic brothers? If not, what keeps you from forming such relationships?

Praying with Scripture
"The Scripture says, 'No one who believes in him will be put to shame'" (Rom 10:11).

THURSDAY
WE NEED TO BE MEN WHO ACT ON THE WORD WE HEAR

Therefore, my beloved, as you have always obeyed, so now, not only as in my presence but much more in my absence, work out your own salvation with fear and trembling; for God is at work in you, both to will and to work for his good pleasure. Do all things without grumbling or questioning, that you may be blameless and innocent, children of God without blemish in the midst of a crooked and perverse generation, among whom you shine as lights in the world, holding fast the word of life, so that in the day of Christ I may be proud that I did not run in vain or labor in vain.

Philippians 2:12–16

God's grace empowers us to act on his holy teachings according to his will. It is easy to claim to have faith; it is much harder to put that faith into practice. Yet a faith that does not act is not a living faith. Living faith opens us up to say yes to God's call to salvation, a call we must answer with fear and trembling. Only with living, active faith can we surrender in trust to God's guidance over our lives.

Jesus gives us the grace to say yes to his call and to turn our faith into actions that transform our world through sacrificial love. We are the eyes, ears, hands, and feet of Christ, carrying out his work through the Church in a broken world. Our salvation is both personal and communal, a past event and an ongoing journey to a final destination. As Catholic men, we wrap our heads around these truths by learning to love others as Jesus has loved us.

Questions for Reflection
Why is faith without living works of love nothing more than dead faith? Does your faith live through loving works? If not,

how can you begin to change that?

Who helps you live a godly life as a Catholic man? Are there other men you seek out? If not, how can you change that?

What acts of love have you offered to those around you who are hurting and lost?

Praying with Scripture
"For we are his workmanship, created in Christ Jesus for good works, which God prepared beforehand, that we should walk in them" (Eph 2:10).

FRIDAY
WE CAN LOOK DEEPLY INTO GOD'S PERFECT LAW AND BE SET FREE TO LOVE

Now the Lord is the Spirit, and where the Spirit of the Lord is, there is freedom. And we all, with unveiled face, beholding the glory of the Lord, are being changed into his likeness from one degree of glory to another; for this comes from the Lord who is the Spirit.

2 Corinthians 3:12–18

In Christ we behold the face of Love! The veil that covered the Holy of Holies in the ancient temple has been torn asunder, giving us access to the very glory of the Almighty. In Christ, freedom has replaced fear. Because of his great sacrificial love, we have been set free from the darkness of doubt and uncertainty. Now we can come boldly before God's throne to find mercy and receive the grace we need for godly living (cf. Heb 4:16).

Christ sets us free from sin and empowers us to live out our faith and become a blessing to the world. We are daily being transformed into the image of Christ, the One who loved the world to the fullest. We Catholic men must cast aside our fear and doubt and commit to a single-minded, passionate, and ever-growing relationship with Christ. We must take the transforming faith we experience day by day and carry it to the lost of this world. We must become better men, better husbands, better fathers, and better brothers in the Faith. We must move from glory to glory, through the trials by the transforming power of the cross, so that we can bring change and renewal to this world. Nothing else will do for those who are truly sold-out for Christ.

Questions for Reflection

How has the love of Christ opened your eyes to your potential to love others in his name?

What is one specific area where you have seen the transforming power of love in your life?

Where would you like to see growth in your Christian walk in the coming weeks?

Praying with Scripture

"As face mirrors face in water, so the heart reflects the person" (Prv 27:19, NABRE).

SATURDAY

Go Deeper

How has God revealed my worth to me this week? Do I believe that he is the sole source of my worthiness?

_____

_____

_____

_____

_____

What obstacles bring doubt and keep me from living my faith more fully?

_____

_____

_____

_____

Am I willing to recognize and accept my lowliness before God, or do I resist it? If I am resistant, what holds me back? Is it fear? Pride? Doubt?

_____

_____

_____

_____

What doubts and fears toss me around and lead me away from God's steady, transforming love?

_____

_____

_____

_____

_____

Have I intentionally neglected to be a doer of the Word this week? Where was I negligent? How can I be more generous in the coming weeks?

_____

_____

_____

_____

Have I allowed my struggles this week to lead me into a deeper relationship with God and with my brothers? If not, what stood in the way? Who are one or two men I can trust to help me through the trials God sends my way?

_____

_____

_____

_____

WEEK 3

COMMON TATERS ON THE AXE

Jesus answered and said to him, "Amen, amen, I say to you, no one can see the kingdom of God without being born from above." Nicodemus said to him, "How can a person once grown old be born again? Surely he cannot reenter his mother's womb and be born again, can he?" Jesus answered, "Amen, amen, I say to you, no one can enter the kingdom of God without being born of water and Spirit. What is born of flesh is flesh, and what is born of spirit is spirit. Do not be amazed that I told you, 'You must be born from above.' The wind blows where it wills, and you can hear the sound it makes, but you do not know where it comes from or where it goes; so it is with everyone who is born of the Spirit."

John 3:3–8 (NABRE)

There is a scene in one of Laura Ingalls Wilder's *Little House on the Prairie* books where the whole town is gathered at the schoolhouse for an evening of entertainment. During the last round of a game of charades, Pa Ingalls walks to the front of the room with a couple of potatoes balanced on the head of an axe. No one can figure out what the phrase is. Finally, Pa says, "It's Common Taters on the Axe!" — Commentators on the Acts (of the Apostles). It is so clever and yet so simple that everyone misses the point.

When Nicodemus came to Jesus at night, our Lord presented him with "common taters": a no-nonsense answer to the deepest longing in Nicodemus's heart. It was simple and direct, something a child would be able to grasp. Yet the phrase about being born used in the passage has a double meaning. It can be translated as "born again" or "born from above." As a result, Nicodemus became confused about the kind of rebirth Jesus was really offering him. This great teacher of the law was unable to grasp the simple truth that Jesus had come to bring us new birth in him.

Catholic men are often equally slow to learn the simple truth of what it means to believe in Jesus. We are self-reliant, intellectual, strong-willed adults who try so hard to be men of faith that we miss the point of what having faith is all about. Jesus, in his conversation with Nicodemus, has the fresh ideas we need. Consider the following:

1. We often complicate what is very simple and fail to act in God's way.

As Catholics, we often focus so hard on understanding our faith that we stumble over the most basic of truths. This can cause us to respond to others with an air of superiority, or to fail to act to change our world. We must remember that Jesus offers us truths that are absolutely profound, but also simple enough for any child to understand.

2. "Amen, Amen" means to pay attention.

Twice in his meeting with Nicodemus, Jesus says to him, "Amen, amen." This was to let Nicodemus — and all of us — know how critical it is for us to accept this truth about being born from above. It is crucial for understanding what his death on the cross and our salvation are all about. Without this clarity, we may forget that we are called to live in such a way as to bring the power and presence of heaven into the lives of those around us.

3. We do not live according to the flesh.

Jesus came in the flesh to bring salvation from above. We are called to see beyond our senses to understand the workings of God in our lives, our Church, and our world. Being born from above means we see life through the lens of heaven and live out in the fullest way possible the kingdom of God in the here and now. True rebirth in Christ is a matter of the spirit and a matter of faith carried out in actions that reflect God's perfect Law of Love.

4. There is no other way to heaven.

The resurrection life and the perfect love of Christ take us a lifetime to learn as we work out our journey to heaven one trembling step at a time. If we fail to be men who are truly born from above, we will fail to build the kingdom of God and draw others into the Church. We must live and act for God's purposes, for no other way will bring us to our home.

5. The wind of the Spirit blows where it will.

We cannot grasp how the Holy Spirit works, how the sacraments bring us grace, or how God takes our weakness and turns it into his strength. Yet we know that all these things are the power that moves us to will and to act according to God's good purposes. Knowing the Spirit of God works out all things to the good allows us to move with the freedom that can come only from perfect trust. That is how we build the kingdom, day by day.

This Week's Call to Action

This week let all your actions reflect the simple truth of John 3:16: "For God so loved the world that he gave his only-begotten Son, that whoever believes in him should not perish but have eternal life." God's perfect love was made manifest in the Incarnation and found its fulfillment on the cross. Put aside your struggle to believe in Christ's love and cast away your self-condemnation or self-aggrandizement. Surrender to this great love so that you can share it with others who so desperately need it.

SUNDAY

Surrendering to Christ and the salvation he won for us must be the foundation for our actions as Catholic men. We are called not just to express our faith in words, but to live it out in the real world, ministering to others and building up the Body of Christ.

This week ask God for the grace to rediscover (or perhaps to discover for the first time) the incredible Good News of Jesus Christ. The Mass is all about this Good News. Our Sunday worship presents us with the truth of the gospel, that God so loved the world that he gave his only-begotten Son to be the sacrifice for our sins. This Good News spills forth during the Liturgy of the Word. We hear it in the prayers throughout the celebration of the Mass. And we see it most clearly in the Eucharist, where we come face to face with the reality of the love of God touching our lives through the sacrifice of the cross.

This Sunday pray and reflect about what it means to be a believer in Jesus. Consider how being a Catholic is all about accepting that there is no other way to heaven but the cross. Speak honestly to God about the times you have failed to stand up for this truth. Pray a prayer of commitment to Christ, sharing how you will work to deepen your faith and share that faith with others in the weeks to come.

Questions for Reflection
What simple truths of our Faith are you most prone to overcomplicate?

Do you recognize the gospel of Christ as truly Good News? If not, what do you need to do to pull back the veil and see it for what it is?

Do you easily share this Good News with others, not just in words but in your actions? How can you share with greater generosity and joy?

Praying with Scripture

"Truly, I say to you, whoever does not receive the kingdom of God like a child shall not enter it" (Lk 18:17).

MONDAY
WE OFTEN COMPLICATE WHAT IS VERY SIMPLE AND FAIL TO ACT IN GOD'S WAY

At that time the disciples came to Jesus, saying, "Who is the greatest in the kingdom of heaven?" And calling to him a child, he put him in the midst of them, and said, "Truly, I say to you, unless you turn and become like children, you will never enter the kingdom of heaven. Whoever humbles himself like this child, he is the greatest in the kingdom of heaven. Whoever receives one such child in my name receives me."

Matthew 18:1–5

Our nature as men is to want to be in control of our lives. We strive to be the best at all we do, to be knowledgeable about everything, to be masters of our worlds. But in the process of striving to be the best of the best, we often complicate many areas of our lives that in reality are very simple. This also applies to what we believe. Granted, it is important to understand our Catholic Faith and the teachings of the Church as clearly as possible. However, if we are not careful, our pride and self-importance may cause us to focus so much on the particulars of our religion that we stumble over the simplest doctrines of our faith and fail to act for the Kingdom of God.

The wonder and beauty of Christianity is that Jesus has revealed himself to us in a way any child could grasp. Nicodemus, the great teacher of his day, misunderstood the meaning of the phrase *gennatha anothen* (or its Aramaic equivalent) from John 3:3. He believed it to mean "born again," when Jesus meant "born from above."[2] Nicodemus tried to complicate a matter that was simple, and it kept him from drawing nearer to Christ. Jesus was telling him that the real birth of salvation comes from heaven. It is something utterly mysterious, yet it is as simple as the faith of a child. Jesus came to call all people to approach him with childlike innocence and perfect trust. Only then can we grasp the beautiful realities of our faith with our hearts and share them with others in loving and practical ways.

Questions for Reflection

In what ways do you tend to make your Catholic Faith more complicated than it needs to be?

Are there areas of Catholic teaching that you struggle to understand or accept? What are they?

What prevents you from responding to God's invitation with childlike faith? Do you want to have the faith of a child, or do you struggle with this concept?

Praying with Scripture

"Let the children come to me, do not hinder them; for to such belongs the Kingdom of God" (Mk 10:14b).

TUESDAY
"AMEN, AMEN" MEANS TO PAY ATTENTION

"You shall therefore lay up these words of mine in your heart and in your soul; and you shall bind them as a sign upon your

---

2. From the *Ignatius Catholic Study Bible, New Testament*, the Gospel According to Saint John 3:3, 'anew: The Greek expression can mean either 'again' or 'from above.' Nicodemus takes it to mean 'again,' as though Jesus required a physical rebirth to enter his kingdom. This is a misunderstanding. Jesus instead calls for a spiritual rebirth 'from above' (CCC 526). The Greek expression always means 'from above' elsewhere in John (3:31; 19:11, 23).'

hand, and they shall be as frontlets between your eyes. And you shall teach them to your children, talking of them when you are sitting in your house, and when you are walking by the way, and when you lie down, and when you rise. And you shall write them upon the doorposts of your house and upon your gates, that your days and the days of your children may be multiplied in the land which the Lord swore to your fathers to give them, as long as the heavens are above the earth."

Deuteronomy 11:18–21

It can be tempting to take our faith for granted, especially if we have been Catholic our entire lives. Too often, living out our faith can become routine and ritualistic.

Jesus often used the phrase, "Amen, amen, I say to you" as a way to put special emphasis on a holy truth. It was as if he was saying, "Sit up and pay attention to this!" Jesus wanted his followers — including us today — to understand that believing in him is a serious matter. There can be no halfway disciples. Christianity is an all-in endeavor. In order to be members of the Mystical Body who act faithfully on behalf of the Church, we must be born from above, changed into new creations by the saving death of Jesus. There are no shortcuts or substitutions, heroic deeds or magic words that can accomplish what only the cross has done.

The question we Catholic men must ask ourselves is this: *Am I all-in for the cause of Christ?* Are we living as all-in, radically changed, intensely joyful believers? Has the "Amen, amen!" of Jesus penetrated our minds and stirred our souls toward actions that truly manifest the glory, the power, and the presence of Christ to others? Is our faith a living faith, in which the words of the gospel find their fullness in our words, our actions, and the direction our lives take for the kingdom of God? It makes all the difference in the world.

Questions for Reflection

Are you an all-in disciple of Christ, or are there still areas in your life where you hold back?

Are you living out the reality of the gospel in a radical, joyfully committed way?

Praying with Scripture
"For we share in Christ, if only we hold our first confidence firm to the end, while it is said, 'Today, when you hear his voice, do not harden your hearts as in the rebellion'" (Heb 3:14–15).

WEDNESDAY
WE DO NOT LIVE ACCORDING TO THE FLESH

So then, brethren, we are debtors, not to the flesh, to live according to the flesh—for if you live according to the flesh you will die, but if by the Spirit you put to death the deeds of the body you will live.

Romans 8:12–13

We live out our Catholic Faith in our mortal bodies, but we must not live according to the flesh. The body is good, but in our weakness we tend to elevate the desires and inclinations of our body over the needs of our souls. Jesus overcame the sinful tendency of the flesh by living a perfect life and dying a sacrificial death on our behalf. Those who live in Christ have been given the power to crucify the "old man" and be freed from the slavery of sin (Rom 6:6).

To be reborn as a believer in Jesus Christ is a matter of the Spirit. We are called to live by the Spirit in order that we may reflect the love of Christ to the world. How will others recognize Christ if our actions reflect the fallen world in which we live? Our every word and deed must show forth the love of Jesus and the message of salvation. We must live as the new creations we are, shining as examples of faith, loving others sacrificially, and renewing the Church as the Bride of Christ as we reach out to the lost world and draw others into the kingdom of God.

Questions for Reflection

Where in your life do you still struggle to live according to the Spirit, not according to the flesh?

How has the Holy Spirit helped you put to death works of the flesh and show forth the power and presence of Christ to a lost and hurting world?

How can you give support and encouragement to another man who may be struggling to live according to the Spirit right now?

Praying with Scripture

"But the fruit of the Spirit is love, joy, peace, patience, kindness, goodness, faithfulness, gentleness, self-control; against such there is no law" (Gal 5:22–23).

THURSDAY
THERE IS NO OTHER WAY TO HEAVEN

Then Peter, filled with the Holy Spirit, said to them, "Rulers of the people and elders, if we are being examined today concerning a good deed done to a cripple, by what means this man has been healed, be it known to you all, and to all the people of Israel, that by the name of Jesus Christ of Nazareth, whom you crucified, whom God raised from the dead, by him this man is standing before you well. This is the stone which was rejected by you builders, but which has become the cornerstone. And there is salvation in no one else, for there is no other name under heaven given among men by which we must be saved."

Acts 4:8–12

Jesus told his disciples that he is the way to heaven (cf. Jn 14:6). The love of God manifested itself in this world in the person of Christ and brought us salvation through his death on the cross. There is no other way to heaven, yet sadly, even some Christians give in to the lie that there are many ways to heaven outside the Church. The truth is, we cannot have it both ways. We cannot call ourselves believers in Jesus Christ and accept that there are multiple ways to heaven. This fundamental truth must be foundational in how we respond to this broken world and to the lost who will challenge our faith. We must hold on to this reality and stand strong as we share the gospel with others by our words and actions. We cannot call Jesus Lord if we do not believe his words are true and live according to them.

As Catholic men, we must take a stand as Peter did, and proclaim, not just in words but in our deeds, that salvation is found in none other than Jesus Christ. If we really believe this then we must be willing to spend our lives working out our salvation with fear and trembling (cf. Phil 2:12) and learning to love the One who loved us with his life. Being Christian means sharing our faith through acts of love. In a world of growing moral and spiritual relativism, it is all the more important for Catholic men to be bearers of truth to all humanity, no matter what the cost.

Questions for Reflection
How often do you hear that there are numerous ways of attaining salvation? When are you most tempted to believe this?

Are you willing to stand strong in your faith and live by the truth that Jesus is the only way to heaven?

How can you support other men in standing firm in their faith this week?

Praying with Scripture
"Truly, truly, I say to you, he who hears my word and believes

him who sent me, has eternal life; he does not come into judgment, but has passed from death to life" (Jn 5:24).

FRIDAY
THE WIND OF THE SPIRIT BLOWS WHERE IT WILL

When the day of Pentecost had come, they were all together in one place. And suddenly a sound came from heaven like the rush of a mighty wind, and it filled all the house where they were sitting. And there appeared to them tongues as of fire, distributed and resting on each one of them. And they were all filled with the Holy Spirit and began to speak in other tongues, as the Spirit gave them utterance.

Acts 2:1–4

We cannot see the wind as it blows around us, but we can certainly see its effects. So it is with the Holy Spirit. We cannot comprehend the will of God as it moves upon our lives, but we experience its effects the more we try to live as he asks us to live. In a similar way, we do not usually sense the way the Sacraments of Confession and the Eucharist impact us, but over time we see how they transform us. It is only as the events of our lives unfold that we come to a dim understanding of how God is working all things out to the good (cf. Rom 8:28).

The Apostles found freedom and power through the Holy Spirit to go forth boldly to proclaim the gospel to all the world. As we surrender to the power of the Holy Spirit, we too become caught up in the flow of God's power and are moved along as gospel agents of holy transformation. As we go forth to build the kingdom, loving sacrificially, sharing God's truth in love, and meeting the needs of the lost, lives are changed, the Church grows, and God's purposes are fulfilled in the working out of our salvation and our outreach to those in need of this great hope.

Questions for Reflection
Where have you seen evidence of the Holy Spirit working in your life?

In what specific ways do you see the Holy Spirit leading the Church today?

How is the Holy Spirit moving you to have influence in the lives of others?

Praying with Scripture
"And when he had said this, he breathed on them, and said to them, 'Receive the Holy Spirit'" (Jn 20:22).

SATURDAY

Go Deeper
Where have I seen the truth of John 3:16 ("For God so loved the world … ") in my life this week? Do I believe and accept that God loves me that much?

_____

_____

_____

Do I recognize the simplicity of the Good News, or do I tend to overcomplicate it? Where do I need to ask God to help me develop the faith of a child?

_____

_____

_____

_____

_____

Am I sincerely living out the truth that there is no other way to heaven but Jesus Christ? What "other ways" have I tried to follow in my life? What "other ways" am I tempted to follow now?

_____

_____

_____

_____

Do I surrender myself to the Spirit so that I can live out his purposes and build the kingdom in all I say and do? Where do I deliberately neglect or refuse to surrender?

_____

_____

_____

Have I reached out to others with the uncompromising truth of the gospel this week?

_____

_____

WEEK 4

THEN AND NOW

Brethren, I do not consider that I have made it my own; but one thing I do, forgetting what lies behind and straining forward to what lies ahead, I press on toward the goal for the prize of the upward call of God in Christ Jesus.

Philippians 3:13–14

We tend to rewrite our own histories. We often look back on our lives with nostalgia, pining after what we remember as happier days — the simpler times before our mistakes and missteps, our failures and falls from grace. We sometimes wish we could have a "do-over," going back and living our lives knowing what we know now. That kind of regret can kill our spirits and keep us from moving forward in our journeys as Catholic men.

Saint Paul certainly could have dwelt on the past. He was a highly educated leader in his day, an up-and-coming Pharisee who was moving in all the right circles. Yet an encounter with the Risen Lord on the road to Damascus changed everything for him. After that, he faced persecution, physical pain, loneliness, and depression. But he also experienced the joy of seeing many souls won for Christ, the strengthening of his faith through fiery trials, ecstatic visions of heaven, and deep and lasting friendships with other believers. Rather than cling to his former safe and sinful life, he pressed on, longing with all his heart to finish the race and receive the prize of Christ.

God will do the same with us, if we let him. He wants to mold men who will build his Church and lead it into eternity. He wants men who will be strong husbands and fathers, faithful brothers, and solid kingdom servants. For every moment we spend on this earth, God offers us opportunities to grow and shape the world through faithful lives. Yes, we fail, and yes, we have regrets; but our God is powerful enough and loving enough to remake our lives in the image of his Son.

In our journey to heaven we Catholic men have a lot to face — and a lot to gain. This week we will consider these points:

1. We cannot go back, but we can have a fresh start.

Remember: "Therefore, if any one is in Christ, he is a new creation; the old has passed away, behold, the new has come" (2 Cor 5:17). If we have surrendered our lives to Christ and confessed our sins, those past mistakes are truly gone. We do not have to dwell on them anymore. What lies ahead is better than anything that has come before. Heaven will be glorious!

2. The past, no matter how bad, is worked out for the good for those who believe.

As Romans 8:28 says, "We know that in everything God works for good with those who love him, who are called according to his purpose." There is no amount of failure that God cannot turn to success for those who answer his call. God's sovereign purpose for our lives and his Church will prevail in the end.

3. God has wonderful plans for us.

Remember: "For I know the plans I have for you, says the LORD, plans for welfare and not for evil, to give you a future and a hope" (Jer 29:11). God wants to prosper us spiritually and place us on a path to a hopeful future with him.

4. We must carry out without worry the task we have been given.

Paul reminded Timothy: "Let no one despise your youth, but set the believers an example in speech and conduct, in love, in faith, in purity" (1 Tm 4:12). God will equip us also for our role in his Church. All we need to do is be faithful to our calling in Christ.

5. We know the end of the story — it all works out.

"And he who sat upon the throne said, "Behold, I make all things new"" (Rv 21:5a). That same salvation story works itself out in our daily lives. Because of Christ, we can find newness in each day, forgiveness, peace, and a fresh start.

This Week's Call to Action

No matter what you are facing today — family problems, sinful struggles, regrets, or unfulfilled dreams — God can and will bring good out of it all. God can change our hearts, renew our lives, and guide us as we live out our calling as Catholic men. This week meditate on the fact that, in Christ, you are a new creation. This is not just some catchy phrase. It is an eternal truth that is yours because you are part of the Body of Christ. Let every word you speak and every action you carry out reflect the trust, the peace, and the love that come from an intimate relationship with our Lord. See your Christian living in terms of becoming all that God is calling you to be.

There are many men out there experiencing the same struggles that we face. We are called to share the hope we have in Christ. We need to pass along the incredible truth that God works miracles in the most stubborn, sinful, and struggling souls, including ours. Let us be willing to witness with our lives to others, to walk the road to Christ with those who need a Savior, and to remind those who have forgotten their faith what being a Catholic man is all about.

SUNDAY

This week we will meditate on what it means to let go of the past in order to embrace God's plan for our lives. To do this we must accept that we cannot change the past, and trust that God can use our past to change us. God works all things out to the good for those who love him and answer his call. Challenge yourself this week to replace worry with wonder and face trials with trust. Allow the great story of salvation to draw you into a deeper relationship with Christ.

This Sunday, as you attend Mass, let the Liturgy of the Word shape the story of your life. As you hear the readings from Scripture, consider the total story of salvation. From eternity God had you in mind as part of his plan to redeem the world through the cross. When you join in the celebration of the Eucharist, meditate on that perfect moment when heaven and earth were reconciled by the sacrifice of Christ. As you receive the Eucharist, consider how you are participating in the plan of God, made specifically for you so that you can give God glory through your life.

The Eucharist is the celebration of Christ remembering our sins no more, redeeming our mortal bodies, and drawing us into an ever-deepening relationship with the Father and one another.

Questions for Reflection

What parts of your past do you struggle to let go of? How can you start to release them to God's sovereign plan today?

Do you believe that God can work all things for good, even your past mistakes? If not, what keeps you from this great truth?

How can you encourage another man who may be struggling to surrender his past mistakes to God?

Praying with Scripture

"And I am sure that he who began a good work in you will bring it to completion at the day of Jesus Christ" (Phil 1:6).

MONDAY
WE CANNOT GO BACK, BUT WE CAN HAVE A FRESH START

Behold, the days are coming, says the LORD, when I will make a new covenant with the house of Israel and the house of Judah, not like the covenant which I made with their fathers when I took them by the hand to bring them out of the land of Egypt, my covenant which they broke, and I showed myself their Master, says the LORD. But this is the covenant which I will make with the house of Israel after those days, says the LORD: I will put my law within them, and I will write it upon their hearts; and I will be their God, and they shall be my people. And no longer shall each man teach his neighbor and each his brother, saying, "Know the LORD," for they shall all know me, from the least of them to the greatest, says the LORD; for I will forgive their iniquity, and I will remember their sin no more.

Jeremiah 31:31–34

Each of us has a painful past. We all regret things we did out of ignorance and arrogance, a lustful eye, or a prideful heart. Many Catholic men live with these regrets hidden deep inside. We lock them away for fear that exposing our sins will lead to humiliation, rejection, and personal ruin. But in Christ God offers us a new covenant, in which our past sins are remembered no more and we can grow in a profound and intimate relationship with him. God chooses to write his law directly on our hearts, to call us his own, and to make us grow in our faith.

While it can be hard to let go of the past, Jesus has given us the Sacrament of Confession to cleanse us and the Eucharist to nourish us. We have the living Word of God and the teachings of the Church to guide us, and brothers and sisters who will walk beside us as we journey together toward our heavenly home. In Christ we have the joy of making a fresh start as we wave goodbye to the past and behold the new that is to come.

Questions for Reflection

What parts of your painful past are you withholding from God? Why is it hard for you to surrender?

How can you open yourself to God's new covenant and allow his law to be written on your heart?

How can you help other Catholic men let go of their pasts and embrace God's forgiveness?

Praying with Scripture

"For behold, I create new heavens and a new earth; and the former things shall not be remembered or come into mind" (Is 65:17).

TUESDAY
THE PAST, NO MATTER HOW BAD, IS WORKED OUT FOR THOSE WHO BELIEVE

Since we have the same spirit of faith as he had who wrote, "I believed, and so I spoke," we too believe, and so we speak, knowing that he who raised the Lord Jesus will raise us also with Jesus and bring us with you into his presence. For it is all for your sake, so that as grace extends to more and more people it may increase thanksgiving, to the glory of God.

2 Corinthians 4:13–15

Some men are reluctant to come to Christ because they feel

they have gone too far in their sin. They believe they have crossed a sacred line and committed the unpardonable sin — that they are no longer worthy of God's love. In one sense, this is correct. All of us, by the sin of Adam and our own personal sins, have fallen short of the glory of God and are unworthy of his love. God, however, loves us still. He chose to make us worthy through the sacrificial death of Christ on the cross.

Our sins, our sufferings, and our sadness are part of our fallen human nature. Yet in Christ we have the power to overcome our past and experience the life God has given us. There is nothing we have done that God cannot undo, no failure he cannot turn into success for his glory. God will not allow any experience in our lives to go to waste. On the contrary, everything we undergo can help shape us into his image. Our wounds make us better healers; our sufferings make us more sympathetic. Our struggles and our stains help us to walk the road to heaven with others. In the end, if we are willing to surrender our past to his goodness, God's eternal purposes for our lives will find victory.

Questions for Reflection

How has God shown you that you are worthy and beautiful in his sight? Do you believe him?

Where in your life have you seen God turn your past mistakes to good? Do you trust that he will continue to do so?

How can you help another man to discover his worth and purpose in God's plan, no matter what mistakes he may have made?

Praying with Scripture

"For this slight momentary affliction is preparing for us an eternal weight of glory beyond all comparison, because we look not to the things that are seen but to the things that are unseen; for the things that are seen are transient, but the things that are unseen are eternal" (2 Cor 4:17–18).

WEDNESDAY
GOD HAS WONDERFUL PLANS FOR US

The plans of the mind belong to man,
*   but the answer of the tongue is from the LORD.*
All the ways of a man are pure in his own eyes,
*   but the LORD weighs the spirit.*
Commit your work to the LORD
*   and your plans will be established.*

Proverbs 16:1–3

There are quite a few preachers on television these days offering a "prosperity gospel" to their followers. They cite Scripture as "proof" that God desires to provide us with health, wealth, and popularity. This, however, is not what God intended for our lives. He wants to give us so much more than earthly happiness. His plan is for us to become the men he created us to be so that we can bring glory to him. He wants us to be strong, principled, and courageous men of integrity who honor him by all we say and do. He does not promise us wealth, health, or fame. But he *does* promise us the strength to persevere through our trials, and his presence to guide and uplift us every step of the way on the journey of salvation.

Certainly God will send us many blessings throughout our lives. But that does not keep us from suffering. We live in a fallen world, and we will face heartache and pain. We may even face persecution and rejection for what we believe. The good news is that in all this, God will never abandon us. He will give us hope and joy. He will use the fire of our trials to perfect us like gold in a furnace. When we sin he will forgive us and renew us time and time again. He will move us deeper into faith as we grow in the knowledge of his eternal truth and share that truth with those around us. That is the awesome prosperity that God offers to those who believe!

Questions for Reflection

Have you ever felt abandoned by God, as though he did not care about your needs? Do you feel that way now?

In what specific ways has God blessed you, both materially and spiritually?

Where do you see God moving you in his wonderful plan for your life?

Praying with Scripture

"For whatever is born of God overcomes the world; and this is the victory that overcomes the world, our faith" (1 Jn 5:4).

THURSDAY
WE MUST CARRY OUT WITHOUT WORRY THE TASK WE HAVE BEEN GIVEN

Though we speak thus, yet in your case, beloved, we feel sure of better things that belong to salvation. For God is not so unjust as to overlook your work and the love which you showed for his sake in serving the saints, as you still do. And we desire each one of you to show the same earnestness in realizing the full assurance of hope until the end, so that you may not be sluggish, but imitators of those who through faith and patience inherit the promises.
Hebrews 6:9–12

Paul could have claimed many reasons to give in to worry and fear. From the very start God told him that he would suffer much for the sake of the gospel (cf. Acts 9:16). Yet Paul never allowed despair to overcome him. He kept his eyes focused on the cross of Christ and the mission God had given him to do. The early

Christians suffered persecution for their faith, and they were tempted to surrender to worry. The same is true for us today. Yet God calls us to reject worry by keeping our eyes fixed on him as we finish the work he has given us to carry out in our lives.

God will empower and equip us for the role he has ordained we should do. We must remember that we are all members of the Body of Christ, created in Christ Jesus to do good works, which God prepared in advance for us to do (cf. Eph 2:10). Jesus told his followers not to worry but to trust God and to seek the kingdom (cf. Mt 6:25–34). As Catholic men, we have a calling that can find its fulfillment only when we surrender in trust and remain faithful to the One who will see us through it all.

Questions for Reflection

What is something you worry about that you need to surrender to God's loving care? Is there anything that holds you back from surrendering it?

What helps you to stand strong, to trust God, and to persevere in your calling?

What is an area of ministry you see God helping you to fulfill for his glory?

Praying with Scripture

"But seek first his kingdom and his righteousness, and all these things shall be yours as well" (Mt 6:33).

FRIDAY
WE KNOW THE END OF THE STORY — IT ALL WORKS OUT

Then I saw a new heaven and a new earth; for the first heaven and the first earth had passed away, and the sea was no more. And I saw the holy city, new Jerusalem, coming down out of heaven from God, prepared as a bride adorned for her husband; and I heard a great voice from the throne saying, "Behold, the dwelling of God is with men. He will dwell with them, and they shall be his people, and God himself will be with them; he will wipe away every tear from their eyes, and death shall be no more, neither shall there be mourning nor crying nor pain any more, for the former things have passed away."

Revelation 21:1–4

Some people flip to the last page of a novel before they begin so they know how the story turns out. The Bible has given us the last chapter of the story of salvation as encouragement for believers in all generations. We know that in the end we have the victory in Jesus! This hope plays itself out in our daily living and the specific ministries to which God has called us. It guides our words and actions and shapes our hearts. It is the foundation of an ever-renewing faith that captures us and propels us heavenward day by day.

Each moment of our lives fades away so quickly. Though the past is gone, it is a part of who we are and who we are becoming, because God has used it to shape us into men after his own heart. We can rejoice because in Christ each day is new and offers us forgiveness, peace, and the opportunity to start over, working out our salvation by acts of love done with the hope of heaven.

Questions for Reflection

How does knowing the end of our story help you to live out your calling as a believer?

What is one thing from your past that has changed for the better in Christ?

How will the last chapter of our salvation story shape how you love others today?

Praying with Scripture
"For whatever is born of God overcomes the world; and this is the victory that overcomes the world, our faith" (1 Jn 5:4).

SATURDAY

Go Deeper

Where do I struggle to release my past to the mercy of God? What mistakes do I hold on to?

_____

_____

_____

_____

_____

Do I embrace God's work in my life? Where has he worked out for the good even my past sins and mistakes?

_____

_____

_____

_____

_____

Do I cooperate with God's unfolding plan for my life? Where do I resist his plan out of worry, fear, or regret?

_____

_____

_____

_____

_____

Do I live as someone who knows he is a new creation in Christ? How can I live this truth more fully?

_____

_____

_____

_____

Do I trust the One who guides my life? Where is he calling me to trust more deeply?

_____

_____

_____

_____

Do I study God's story? How has the Good News helped me grow in faith?

_____

_____

_____

_____

_____

WEEK 5

GOD'S STILL SMALL VOICE

And he said, "Go forth, and stand upon the mount before the Lord." And behold, the Lord passed by, and a great and strong wind tore the mountains, and broke in pieces the rocks before the Lord, but the Lord was not in the wind; and after the wind an earthquake, but the Lord was not in the earthquake; and after the earthquake a fire, but the Lord was not in the fire; and after the fire a still small voice. And when Elijah heard it, he wrapped his face in his mantle and went out and stood at the entrance of the cave. And behold, there came a voice to him, and said, "What are you doing here, Elijah?"

1 Kings 19:11–13

Men tend to want answers, especially when things are not going right. Not only that, but we usually want our answers to be grand, loud, and larger than life. We want God to move heaven and earth to satisfy our needs. And yet, when we are in our worst moments, that is exactly what we do *not* need!

In the passage above from the First Book of Kings, Elijah had just stood up to the prophets of Baal. He called on God to send down holy fire on his water-soaked sacrifice, and God did as he asked. But then the cruel words of a wicked woman sent him running for his life to hide in a cave. Elijah came to the mountain where God had spoken to Moses, hoping for some great sign to ease his deep despair. He encountered a howling wind, a thundering earthquake, and a raging fire; yet God was not present in any of these signs. Instead, it was the almost inaudible whisper of the Almighty that brought Elijah out of the cave in trembling and awe. God spoke his presence powerfully into Elijah's spirit, offering him comfort, reassurance, and a new sense of purpose. God wants to speak to us in the same way.

What can we, as Catholic men, learn from Elijah's experience? This week we will consider the following:

1. No matter how well things are going, we can stumble at any moment.

Our pride is often our undoing. We need to remember that while God wants to grant us success, we need to remain humble before him. He longs for our obedience and our love more than our valiant efforts. We should always take care, lest we fall (cf. 1 Cor 10:12).

2. God speaks in whispers.

Certainly God has used great signs throughout the ages to show his people who he is. But he usually speaks in simple and subtle ways: through the beauty of creation, in the voices of friends, by little "chance" happenings, through his holy Word, and within the quiet of our hearts. If we are willing to listen to that still small voice, we will hear a great deal.

3. God's answers come in his time and in his way.

Though it was not in the way Elijah expected, God provided the perfect answer to his struggles. He provides unique and unusual miracles in the same way to us today. We may not always understand how God will answer our needs, but we must believe that he will do so each and every time.

4. Our help often comes from people in the Church.

Just as God provided Elijah 7,000 believers who had not bowed down to Baal (cf. 1 Kgs 19:18), he provides us with brothers and sisters in the Church who will lift us up, provide support, and stand with us as we face our struggles and press on to do the work God has called us to do.

5. When God gives his answer, we find new strength.

Elijah found new strength to continue his mission to preach to God's people when he experienced God's answer given in power and love. No great sign is as wonderful as the love of Christ poured out upon our lives.

This Week's Call to Action

As Catholic men, we need to be open, vulnerable, and willing to follow as God leads. This week seek out fellowship with a brother as a way to gain some clarity on your own walk with Jesus. Look for new ways of listening for God's still small voice. Try a new prayer style, take a walk, and listen for the Spirit in the world around you. Hear God speaking to you in your family. Accept that you need Christ to guide you, and allow the Holy Spirit to whisper his wonderful words of hope into your life this week.

Our greatest witness to the gospel is not necessarily in great signs, but in changed lives, in those who are willing to listen to the still small voice of God. As we find strength and renewal in the daily whisperings of heaven's hope, we can work to share this great joy with all we meet. As we become open to the gospel, we will live it out more fully with others.

SUNDAY

Men often look to the things of this world — such as prosperity, position, power, or politics — to resolve the struggles we face and to provide stability and clarity in our lives. But all of these things, even when they appear great, are a vapor compared with the whisper of the Almighty. It is the still small voice of God that speaks the loudest to our searching hearts. Even in the midst of natural disasters, political upheaval, social unrest, and personal tragedy, the quiet presence of God overwhelms all the noise of this life. If we are willing to listen, it will drive us to our knees in wonder and submission.

This Sunday, as you celebrate the Eucharist, let this powerful, seemingly tiny reality shape your perspective on what is truly worthy of wonder. Pray for new eyes to see the silent God present in the Eucharist. Pray for ears to hear his whisper, and let it overflow like a rushing waterfall into your soul. As you listen to God's Word and hear the prayers of Consecration, open your heart to the Spirit's still small voice speaking grace into your soul. Tune your spiritual ears to hear the message of the gospel pouring over you, stirring you to holy action for the kingdom of God.

Questions for Reflection

How has God spoken to you through his still small voice? What keeps you from listening?

How are you answering God's call to witness to others about the joy you have in Christ?

Praying with Scripture

"But they who wait for the LORD shall renew their strength, / they shall mount up with wings like eagles, / they shall run and not be weary, / they shall walk and not faint" (Is 40:31).

MONDAY
NO MATTER HOW WELL THINGS ARE GOING, WE CAN STUMBLE AT ANY MOMENT

Therefore let any one who thinks that he stands take heed lest he fall. No temptation has overtaken you that is not common to man. God is faithful, and he will not let you be tempted beyond

your strength, but with the temptation will also provide the
way of escape, that you may be able to endure it.

1 Corinthians 10:12–13

These days, stories of powerful men falling into sin are all too common. When we witness another's undoing, it is tempting to pass judgment on their failures. But we need to realize that, were it not for Christ, we would be stumbling right there along with them. In fact, all of us have fallen into sin during our lives. Like Elijah, we can be on top of the world, only to experience the worst of who we are as we surrender to sin and fall from grace. The moment we begin to rely on our own strength, we become the most vulnerable to the devil's schemes.

Thankfully we have a Savior who understands our weaknesses perfectly, who was tempted in every way we are and yet never sinned (cf. Heb 4:15). It is through Jesus that we receive the power to overcome our fallen nature and rise above our worldliness.

When we fall, we have the Sacrament of Confession to restore us and bring us back to our community of faith. In Christ we have the grace to avoid the near occasion of any and every sin. As his followers, we need to realize that our Lord longs for our fidelity and trust, rather than our human efforts to tough it out when we are tempted. Without Jesus we will surely fall. With him we can greatly succeed. Let us rejoice in our salvation and the daily bread of God's provision that helps us to continue on our journey to heaven.

Questions for Reflection

Why do we so often listen to the voice of the enemy rather than the voice of our Savior?

How has God raised you from your falls? Where have you experienced his mercy the most?

What practical steps can you take today to avoid temptation

and stand strong in your faith?

Praying with Scripture
"Watch and pray that you may not enter into temptation; the
spirit indeed is willing, but the flesh is weak" (Mt 26:41).

TUESDAY
GOD SPEAKS IN WHISPERS

Now a word was brought to me stealthily,
    my ear received the whisper of it.

Job 4:12

So have no fear of them; for nothing is covered that will not
be revealed, or hidden that will not be known. What I tell you
in the dark, utter in the light; and what you hear whispered,
proclaim upon the housetops.

Matthew 10:26–27

God is ready and willing to speak to hearts weary with failure
and burdened by the guilt of sin. In the midst of his deepest
struggle, Job heard the faintest whisper of truth from the Almighty God, and it brought him trembling to his knees. When
we struggle to be the men we are called to be, we should remember that Jesus longs to step into our lives and respond to our
needs with his perfect, superabundant love. This love may touch
us in the silent reading of the Scriptures, yet it is so powerful that
it will lead us to boldly proclaim the Good News to all the world.
It will reveal the truth of God, draw us away from the road of
destruction, and lead us back to the narrow path to heaven.

As we seek to become the men God calls us to be, God will
speak to us in many ways. He will stir our hearts through his
Word. He will lift us up through the Body of Christ. The sacraments will strengthen us, and the Holy Spirit will whisper his

inspiration into our spiritual ears. We need not look for great and miraculous signs. The greatest sign of Jesus is the cross, where he laid down his life for us in love. As we tune our hearts to listen to that great love, we will hear the still small voice of God gently speaking truth into our lives.

Questions for Reflection

When have you experienced a powerful word from God in a subtle sign? How has it brought you to your knees in awe and wonder?

What has this study been teaching you about crying out to God for deliverance and direction?

How does experiencing the power and presence of the Holy Spirit in God's grace-filled whispers bring you strength and lead you to greater acts of love in his name?

Praying with Scripture

"Behold, these are but the outskirts of his ways; and how small a whisper do we hear of him! But the thunder of his power who can understand?" (Jb 26:14).

WEDNESDAY
GOD ANSWERS IN HIS TIME AND IN HIS WAY

For my thoughts are not your thoughts,
*   neither are your ways my ways, says the LORD.*
For as the heavens are higher than the earth,
*   so are my ways higher than your ways*
*   and my thoughts than your thoughts.*

Isaiah 55:8–9

But do not ignore this one fact, beloved, that with the Lord one

day is as a thousand years, and a thousand years as one day.
The Lord is not slow about his promise as some count slowness,
but is forbearing toward you, not wishing that any should per-
ish, but that all should reach repentance.

2 Peter 3:8–9

We weak human beings have a tendency to present our plans to God and expect him to bless them. Those plans may spring from the best of intentions, but if they are not God's plans, they are empty and meaningless. Just as Elijah came to the mountain expecting God to answer him as he had answered Moses many years before, we often come to God expecting him to respond to our prayers in predictable ways. But God's ways and his timing are all his own, and they are perfect. He will answer us, but in the way and at the time that is truly best for us and for his ultimate glory.

The end game of God's love is the salvation of our souls, the perfection of our hearts, and the completion of our journeys according to his will. We are called to yield to his perfect power, love, and majesty. He is God and we are not. We must trust that his love for us will provide no other answer than the one that is the best for our souls.

Questions for Reflection
When have you brought your plans to God expecting him to bless them? How did that turn out?

When have you yielded your goals and desires to the greater good and the glory of God? What was the result?

How has surrendering to God's will made you a better disciple of Christ?

Praying with Scripture
"Wait for the LORD; / be strong, and let your heart take courage; / yes, wait for the LORD!" (Ps 27:14).

THURSDAY
OUR HELP OFTEN COMES FROM PEOPLE IN THE CHURCH

And let us consider how to stir up one another to love and good works, not neglecting to meet together, as is the habit of some, but encouraging one another, and all the more as you see the Day drawing near.

Hebrews 10:24–25

Elijah thought that he was all alone in his spiritual journey. Often we too feel as though we are on our own. But Jesus left us the Church so that we could receive the help we need to find our way. We have all heard people say, "I don't need to go to church! I can worship God on my own." While we certainly can experience the presence of God wherever we are, we cannot make our way on the path to perfection without the loving help of our brothers and sisters in Christ. Jesus opened the way to heaven and gave us the gift of his Body, his Church, so that we could encourage and lift one another up in love.

Our Baptism came through the Church. When we go to Confession, we are reconciled with God and with the Church. The Church witnesses our marriages and blesses us when we are sick. And in the Eucharist we gather as the Church to celebrate the gift of our salvation through the sacrifice of Jesus on the cross. Many see the Church as an institution that burdens men. The Church is not just an organization, but the Mystical Body of Christ, the hands and feet, eyes and ears of the Savior, reaching out to the world. Through the Church, we receive strength, fellowship, and the grace to overcome the world as we walk on the road to salvation to our heavenly home.

Questions for Reflection
Have you ever tried to walk the Christian walk without the Church to help you? What happened?

When have you received the grace, love, and help you needed through the Church?

How can you respond to those who say they do not need the church?

Praying with Scripture
"Behold, how good and pleasant it is when brothers dwell in unity!" (Ps 133:1).

FRIDAY
WHEN GOD GIVES HIS ANSWER, WE FIND NEW STRENGTH

Ascribe power to God,
whose majesty is over Israel,
and his power is in the skies.
Awesome is God in his sanctuary,
the God of Israel,
he gives power and strength to his people.
Blessed be God!

Psalm 68:34–35

Though God speaks in whispers, his gentle word is full of great power. When we experience an answer to prayer, we find the strength to move forward in our journey of faith. God longs to answer our needs, and his answer, even when it is not what we thought we wanted to hear, gives us the power to accomplish his will and to live as his children.

Our response to God's still small voice should be one of thanksgiving, wonder, and awe. We often take for granted that we are children of an all-loving, all-powerful Father who not only chooses to answer our needs, but really desires to do so. His blessings are always for our good. His love is all we need.

As we experience the awesomeness of God in his works, we should, like Elijah, fall to our knees and surrender ourselves to his calling in our lives.

Questions for Reflection

How have you experienced the strength of God in your life? Have you always experienced his strength in this way?

How would you describe the truth that God is so beyond us and yet so near to our hearts?

What has surrendering to the still small voice of God taught you about serving him?

Praying with Scripture

"He gives power to the faint, and to him who has no might he increases strength" (Is 40:29).

SATURDAY

Go Deeper

Where have I seen God providing strength, wisdom, and peace to me this week? Have I thanked him?

_____

_____

_____

_____

_____

Have I allowed myself to forget that I can stumble at any moment? Where have I slipped into pride in my godly actions?

_____

_____

_____

_____

Do I wait on God to answer my prayers and needs in his time and his way? Where do I struggle with his schedule or his plans?

_____

_____

_____

_____

Do I seek support and wisdom from the Church in guiding my way, or am I trying to make it on my own?

_____

_____

_____

_____

How have I shared God's whispers of love with others through my acts of love?

_____

_____

_____

_____

_____

WEEK 6

BROTHER TO BROTHER

Put on then, as God's chosen ones, holy and beloved, compassion, kindness, lowliness, meekness, and patience, forbearing one another and, if one has a complaint against another, forgiving each other; as the Lord has forgiven you, so you also must forgive. And over all these put on love, which binds everything together in perfect harmony. And let the peace of Christ rule in your hearts, to which indeed you were called in the one body. And be thankful. Let the word of Christ dwell in you richly, as you teach and admonish one another in all wisdom, and as you sing psalms and hymns and spiritual songs with thankfulness in your hearts to God. And whatever you do, in word or deed, do everything in the name of the Lord Jesus, giving thanks to God the Father through him.

Colossians 3:12–17

We need spiritual brothers to be involved in our lives. We need other men who will hold us accountable, confront us about our sin, walk with us on our faith journeys, and lift us up so that we can live fully sold-out for Christ. Left on our own we run the risk of falling into self-reliant, self-centered behavior. We may struggle with temptation and sins of anger, lust, pride, or any other sin. We neglect the Word, our worship, the sacraments, and Church involvement. But when brothers come alongside us, we find the strength to jump back into the game and take our place in the Mystical Body as capable men of integrity and honor.

Developing intimate friendships with other men is not always easy. Sitting down with the guys to watch sports or have a few beers is one thing; but asking a brother to keep us on the narrow path of salvation is quite another. Catholic men often find it hard to make it to Mass on Sundays, let alone dig more deeply into their personal issues or share their feelings with other men. We need to step up. There are men all around us who need a Catholic brother to speak truth and hope into their lives.

While men may have trouble being relational, it is not impossible if we are willing to let down our guard and reach out to others. Believe it or not, most men are looking for other men who will listen and offer support. We who have committed to growing in the truths of our faith can bond with them in many simple ways. Offering help with a home improvement project can get things rolling. Having some "guy time" when we get together with couples is another. And joining together in prayer and study groups opens the door for honest sharing. The more we are willing to be there for them, the more our brothers will want to be there for us.

The calling to live in true communion with our brothers involves some effort. This week we will consider a few ideas on fellowship from the reading from Colossians, quoted at the beginning of this chapter:

1. True manly living requires committed brotherhood.

We cannot simply play the part of a brother. It must be something that is so much a part of our lives that it is as natural as breathing and as powerful as each beat of our hearts. We are called to reach into the brokenness of others' lives in a way that honors their dignity and gives glory to God. Walking with our brothers is a lifelong journey that requires a commitment grounded in the Body of Christ.

2. Our strength lies in meekness.

Words such as "heartfelt compassion, kindness, humility, gentleness, and patience" (Col 3:12) are not "manly" words in the accepted, worldly sense. Yet these are truly powerful virtues that allow us to be strong models of faith to our fellow men.

3. Forgiveness is a foundational blessing.

Men fall, and sometimes we fall hard. Our willingness to forgive one another is so crucial to fellowship. We need to confront one another with our grievances so that we may be reconciled to one another and find healing.

4. Love is the bonding agent of our fellowship.

Love is the glue that holds all the other virtues together. Without the sacrificial love of Christ, our actions are overrun by our selfishness and fear. Love leads us toward perfection, giving grace to all our interactions with our brothers.

5. Christ is the focus, the power, and the goal of our lives.

Jesus must control our lives, energize our actions, and bring richness to our relationships with our brothers and stability to their lives. We must surrender to the headship of Christ, allowing him to direct our plans, we are able to join with our brothers in joyful, meaningful, and thankful fellowship as we serve the One who came to serve and give his life as a ransom for the many.

This Week's Call to Action

The more we live this life of fellowship with the Lord and one another, the more we will align ourselves with God's will and lighten the burden each of us bears, as we walk the road of salvation together. Christians talk about "leading others to Christ." Catholic men not only lead other men to Christ; they equip them, stand by them, and support them every step of the way on their journey toward our heavenly home. True brotherhood is a lifelong process of personal growth, accountability and support, and joyful fellowship shared within the community of the Church.

SUNDAY

This week we will focus on the brotherhood we share with other Catholic men. Love is the glue that binds all things together. This love is centered in the One who came to earth to give his life for us. True brotherhood is all about committing to be a real man: an unafraid, honest, reliable, and loving brother to other Catholic men. We are called to live out this holy purpose, to be shining examples of integrity and godly action within the Church as we build up the Body of Christ and find practical ways to be blessings to other men.

When you spend time in worship this Sunday, rejoice in the fact that you come together with brothers and sisters not only in your local parish, but with believers throughout the world. Keep your brothers in mind as you greet them and pray for them. Take time after Mass to reach out to your brothers and consider specific things you can do to build them up. Let each part of the celebration of the Eucharist remind you how the Savior went to the cross so that you could have fellowship with him and with your family in faith. As you receive the Eucharist, thank God that you have been united with your brothers in the sacrament that is central to our journey as believers and as men.

If you devote time to journaling, make a list of brothers and their needs and plan to pray for them during the week. Think of ways you can encourage them in word and deed, and then follow up on that plan. It could be a text or an email, sitting down for coffee, helping with a project, or taking a hike or jog together. Whatever you do, let it build up your fellowship and friendship.

Questions for Reflection

Who are the men in your life who are walking this road to heaven with you?

How can you come alongside other men in your life and support them on their journeys?

What are the most important ways in which you need support? How can you ask for it?

Praying with Scripture

"Iron sharpens iron, and one man sharpens another" (Prv 27:17).

MONDAY
TRUE MANLY LIVING REQUIRES COMMITTED BROTHERHOOD

We know that we have passed out of death into life, because we love the brethren. He who does not love remains in death. Any one who hates his brother is a murderer, and you know that no murderer has eternal life abiding in him. By this we know love, that he laid down his life for us; and we ought to lay down our lives for the brethren. But if any one has the world's goods and sees his brother in need, yet closes his heart against him, how does God's love abide in him? Little children, let us not love in word or speech but in deed and in truth.

1 John 3:14–18

Being a true Christian brother means we cannot remain passive. Living virtuously with our brothers is not just a matter of well wishes and kind words. Christianity is an encounter between a broken world and the Risen Christ, as we work together to overcome the death of sin and build one another up in the strength of the Lord. Catholic men are called to love their brothers deeply, intimately, and solidly — not just with pleasantries and common interests, but with true concern for their ultimate destination. It may mean facing tough times, and it always requires openness and vulnerability on our part.

The Catholic Faith is not for the weak-minded. It is not something to which we half-heartedly commit. We are called to be a band of brothers, marching onward toward victory in Christ, lifting one another up as together we carry out the cause of the gospel. We must commit to loving, honoring, and serving our brothers, because if we fail to support our brothers in the Faith, we will all fall when troubles and trials present themselves. Starting today let us commit to standing with our brothers, so that we can support one another in giving ourselves fully to the Lord.

Questions for Reflection

How connected are you to your brothers? Do you strive to walk with them, to serve them, and to help them on their journeys?

How can you give strength today to a brother who needs your support?

Praying with Scripture

"For as many of you as were baptized into Christ have put on Christ" (Gal 3:27).

TUESDAY
OUR STRENGTH LIES IN MEEKNESS

Submit yourselves therefore to God. Resist the devil and he will flee from you. Draw near to God and he will draw near to you.

James 4:7–8

One important aspect of Christian brotherhood is learning to be meek. Men often think that "meek" equals "weak." But being meek means understanding that, on our own, we will never be strong enough to resist temptation, overcome sin, and live a life of virtue. True meekness seeks to yield to the purposes of God and accept the spiritual strength we need from him to grow into the men we were created to be. In Christ we are able to overcome our human weakness by drawing from the wellspring of his power.

We need to get serious and sober about our humble state before God, because we cannot walk with our brothers in truth and stand strong against the trials of life unless we are pure in heart, sold-out in our passion to live like Christ, and temperate in our judgment on all matters pertaining to working out our salvation. Meek brothers are committed to walking with one another every step of the way on our journey to the kingdom.

Questions for Reflection
How hard is it for you to embrace meekness by surrendering your human strength to God?

How does living with a pure heart and a sober mind help you to bring Christ's strength to bear on every circumstance of your life?

What are some specific things you can do today to be an example of meekness to other men?

Praying with Scripture
"He leads the humble in what is right, and teaches the humble his way" (Ps 25:9).

WEDNESDAY
Forgiveness Is a Foundational Blessing

If your brother sins against you, go and tell him his fault, between you and him alone. If he listens to you, you have gained your brother. But if he does not listen, take one or two others along with you, that every word may be confirmed by the evidence of two or three witnesses. If he refuses to listen to them, tell it to the Church; and if he refuses to listen even to the Church, let him be to you as a Gentile and a tax collector. Truly, I say to you, whatever you bind on earth shall be bound in heaven, and whatever you loose on earth shall be loosed in heaven.

Matthew 18:15–18

Confronting sin in our brothers is one of the most difficult aspects of living a Christian life. Society and culture tell us that we should have the freedom to live our lives the way we see fit without anyone judging us or our decisions. The problem with this is that, ultimately, it isn't a very loving approach toward our brothers in the Faith. Freedom without truth and sin without reconciliation lead to unrighteous living — and that, left unchecked, will lead inevitably to destruction.

While we must leave final judgment up to God, Catholic men are called to recognize sin for what it is, and speak truth into the lives of other men when we see it. From a practical perspective, there are ways we can challenge our brothers to overcome sin without condemning them. Jesus left the Church the means of confronting sin and restoring individuals to fellowship. We can draw from the strength of the Body when we work for unity and reconciliation for all our brothers.

It is important to approach faults in others with gentleness, respect, and humility. We must always remember that we also fall (cf. 1 Cor 10:12). Our focus should be on our concern for our brothers, not with our self-righteous need to prove we are "better" than they are. We need to be ready to explain our position, forgive the hurt, and walk the path of reconciliation. Together we must lift one another up and remain strong as believing brothers, united in the cause of Christ, who calls us to purity and perfection in his name.

Questions for Reflection

When have you had to confront sin in a brother, and how did you handle it? Has a brother ever had to confront you? How did it help you?

What do you do to hold yourself accountable before you point out any sin in another?

What are some practical ways you can help to walk with a brother facing sin today?

Praying with Scripture

"And be kind to one another, tenderhearted, forgiving one another, as God in Christ forgave you" (Eph 4:32).

THURSDAY
LOVE IS THE BONDING AGENT OF OUR FELLOWSHIP

Let love be genuine; hate what is evil, hold fast to what is good; love one another with brotherly affection; outdo one another in showing honor. Never flag in zeal, be aglow with the Spirit, serve the Lord. Rejoice in your hope, be patient in tribulation, be constant in prayer. Contribute to the needs of the saints, practice hospitality.

Romans 12:9–13

Love is everything. Love descended from heaven and took on flesh, walked the dusty roads of Palestine, and went to the cross to redeem the world. Love left us a holy fellowship of believers, guided by the Holy Spirit. Together we live out the call to build one another up in love. Mature Catholic men focus on the eternal purpose for which we were created: to love as God has loved us. We seek to live stable lives of prayer, evangelization, worship, and ministry, with each man doing his part to follow the direction of Jesus our head. As we live out this unity, we build up one another in love.

There is no virtue as perfect, as powerful, and as potent as sacrificial love. It is the spiritual glue that holds together all that we are in Christ. It is the work that completes our faith, the joyful activity that brings to perfection our fellowship and our mission as a community of believers united in the Lord. As we love our families, our Church, and our world, we bring the grace of God to bear upon the universe. As we carry out our call to love our Catholic brothers, we build them up in their faith and grow with them in fellowship, knowledge, and solidarity of purpose.

Questions for Reflection

What has Jesus taught you about how to love others, particularly your Catholic brothers?

Where do you see love working itself out in the life of your local church? What part do you play in this?

How can you help make the love of Christ a greater reality in the life of a brother today?

Praying with Scripture

"I appeal to you, brethren, by the name of our Lord Jesus Christ, that all of you agree and that there be no dissensions among you, but that you be united in the same mind and the same judgment" (1 Cor 1:10).

FRIDAY
CHRIST IS THE FOCUS, THE POWER, AND THE GOAL OF OUR LIVES

For this reason I bow my knees before the Father, from whom every family in heaven and on earth is named, that according to the riches of his glory he may grant you to be strengthened with might through his Spirit in the inner man, and that Christ may dwell in your hearts through faith; that you, being rooted and grounded in love, may have power to comprehend with all the saints what is the breadth and length and height and depth, and to know the love of Christ which surpasses knowledge, that you may be filled with all the fulness of God.

Ephesians 3:14–19

Christ cannot live on the outskirts of our lives. He is the truest brother who sets the perfect example we are to follow. He must be the center of all we are, and that includes our relationships with our brothers. As we root our lives in him, we grow in his perfect love, the love that is beyond our human understanding. When Jesus is our all in all, we experience the fullness of our Christian life and are set free to love our brothers with the same perfect love with which he has loved us.

We must focus our whole lives on the journey to heaven. Together with our brothers, we must take up our cross and follow in the steps of our Savior, seeking his example and his power, and moving ever forward in faith. The more we seek God's fullness and strive to live as he has called us, the more we are strengthened and united to our brothers. Together we become who we were meant to be, building one another up and discovering the wonder of our Catholic life in Christ.

Questions for Reflection
How has becoming more deeply rooted in the love of Christ changed your friendships with others?

What areas of your faith do you need to strengthen, and how can your brothers support you in growing closer to Jesus?

How have you seen the fullness of Christ being manifested in your fellowship with your brothers?

Praying with Scripture
"Behold, how good and pleasant it is when brothers dwell in unity!" (Ps 133:1).

SATURDAY

Go Deeper
How have I made a deeper commitment to seek out and build up my Catholic brothers this week?

_____

_____

_____

_____

Who in my life needs my forgiveness? Have I withheld it for any reason?

_____

_____

_____

_____

Have I worked to foster healthy, honest, and accountable relationships with my Catholic brothers, so that together we can experience more fully the love of Christ manifesting itself in our lives?

_____

_____

_____

_____

_____

_____

Have I called my brothers to better living, especially when I see them falling into sin, or have I kept silent out of fear?

_____

_____

_____

_____

_____

_____

_____

Have I accepted my brothers' words of encouragement, insight, or reproof, and have I spoken the truth to them in love without judgment or unnecessary criticism?

_____

_____

_____

_____

_____

How have I grown in unity with my brothers, joining together to build up the Church as we build up one another?

_____

_____

_____

_____

_____

WEEK 7

You're a Loser!

Then Jesus told his disciples, "If any man would come after me, let him deny himself and take up his cross and follow me. For whoever would save his life will lose it, and whoever loses his life for my sake will find it. For what will it profit a man, if he gains the whole world and forfeits his life? Or what shall a man give in return for his life? For the Son of man is to come with his angels in the glory of his Father, and then he will repay every man for what he has done."

Matthew 16:24–27

Perhaps one of the biggest insults one man can give another is to call him a loser. When we are told that we are the opposite of a successful, purposeful man, it can cut to the core of who we are. We are driven to succeed, to find purpose in our lives, and to be the best that we can be. The message of the cross contradicts our natural inclinations as men. However, Jesus joyfully offers us this blessed paradox: in order to gain eternal life and the treasures of heaven, we have to lose our life.

Why is this? Because the whole world is nothing compared with Christ. In him we find every treasure worth possessing. It is not a burden to give up everything in order to live for Christ; it is a blessing, a holy call given to us out of love. In Christ, being a loser becomes the highest prize imaginable!

This week we are going to focus on turning our understanding of loss and gain on its head by considering the following points:

1. Jesus brings not peace, but a sword.

Jesus never promised us an easy, peaceful life. He said that believing in him would divide families. He said that those who would not take up their crosses would be unworthy of him (cf. Mt 10:34–38). He called us to this radical ideal because anyone or anything we love more than God is an idol that leads us away from heaven.

2. We consider all things a loss to gain Christ.

Our love for Christ fills us with such joy that everything else is rubbish compared with our salvation, as Saint Paul said (cf. Phil 3:8). To the world we are fools because we put Christ first. But once we have experienced his saving power and love, especially through our connection with his Body the Church, we see the charms of this world for the false treasures they truly are.

3. There are no participation trophies.

We are told to run the race to win, and to go into strict training to accomplish that goal (cf. 1 Cor 9:24–27). The Christian life is not a spectator sport. We are here to win: to win souls for Christ, to win honor for the Church, and to win heaven for ourselves by living out our faith in love. We don't get a prize merely for participating half-heartedly. We've got to be all-in if we are to cross the finish line and win the prize of heaven. It is all or nothing for Christ.

4. God sticks by those who carry on the fight.

God calls us to be strong and courageous. Though we appear weak and insignificant by worldly standards, we have our heavenly Father on our side. He will never leave us or forsake us (cf. Dt 31:6; Jo 1:9). Therefore, we never need to be afraid of losing, because God gives us his victory.

5. Hope turns weaklings into eagles.
When we accept our weakness and put our trust in the Lord, we find renewed strength to continue the journey. In fact, we soar on wings like eagles. We run without stopping. We walk and do not faint (cf. Is 40:31). In Christ we experience moments of glory, days of passion, and times of refreshment because he is our strength and our victory.

This Week's Call to Action

Real men witness through their weakness, which God turns into strength. We admit our need for God, our connection to the Body of Christ, and our dependence on the Holy Spirit to guide our lives. We exist in a place where God is our ultimate support and strength. By our example we show others that they too can experience the same strength in Jesus.

In the eyes of the world we may appear to be losers. But if we live our radical call with authentic love, our joy will be irresistible. Our witness will draw others to wonder what it is that brings us such joy, and they will want to tap into that same power that fuels our authentic lives. No one ever discovered true joy living merely by worldly standards of success. Remember that when we are caught up in the strength of the Almighty, there is nothing that can stop us.

SUNDAY

This week we will focus on what it means to be a loser in God's economy. Even though faith can lead to division, it also provides us with the solid and stable power that comes from allowing God to be our strength. Our faith is a battle that requires serious training in the Word, sacraments, study, and fellowship if we truly want to win the victory. We who have surrendered to Christ and allowed ourselves to become losers in the world's eyes are the real winners. We are empowered by the Holy Spirit and made into new creations, servant soldiers who carry the call of the gospel with us in all we say and do.

The Word of God that you hear every Sunday at Mass is filled with stories and statements of faith that speak powerfully to the truth that God takes losers and turns them into winners for the gospel. This Sunday, as you listen to the readings from the Scriptures and the Eucharistic Prayer, consider the great story of salvation and how it has been fulfilled in Jesus Christ. Thank God that he has made you an important part of that story. Make a deeper commitment today to follow your heavenly commander's lead and pray for his strength as you carry the message of the gospel with you and share it by all you say and do.

Questions for Reflection

Are you afraid of being considered a loser? Why? In which areas can you ask the Lord to give you his perspective on what it means to lose in order to gain?

Have you had to give up anything in your life in order to gain Christ? What was it that you gave up? Was it worth it?

Praying with Scripture

"But Jesus looked at them and said to them, 'With men this is impossible, but with God all things are possible'" (Mt 19:26).

MONDAY
JESUS BRINGS NOT PEACE, BUT A SWORD

"Do not think that I have come to bring peace on earth; I have not come to bring peace, but a sword. For I have come to set a man against his father, and a daughter against her mother, and a daughter-in-law against her mother-in-law; and a man's foes will be those of his own household. He who loves father or

mother more than me is not worthy of me; and he who loves
son or daughter more than me is not worthy of me; and he who
does not take his cross and follow me is not worthy of me. He
who finds his life will lose it, and he who loses his life for my
sake will find it."

Matthew 10:34–39

These words may sound rather harsh. Some see this passage as exaggerated or symbolic language; but in truth, Jesus speaks clearly and without compromise. If we put anyone or anything before him, we become unworthy of inheriting the kingdom. Jesus is not calling us to hate our families. He is calling us to love him even more. He knows that believing in him can cause deep and painful divisions among family members. Those who would choose the cross will suffer loss on some level, but these are all temporary losses of lesser goods. Losing Christ, on the other hand, is losing an eternal treasure.

The Christian life is not easy, but it is joyful and fulfilling. The sword of division that our Catholic Faith brings can be painful, especially in our world, where many see anything Christian in a negative light. But what the world views as loss is actually eternal gain for those who believe. When we face up to what living in the shadow of the cross means, we discover new life and a peace that surpasses all understanding or expectation. That peace empowers us to live our lives dedicated to the cause of the gospel.

Questions for Reflection
What division have you experienced because of your Catholic Faith?

What is the hardest thing about standing up for Christ in the modern world?

How can you encourage a brother who may be struggling to take up his cross and follow Christ?

Praying with Scripture

"I came to cast fire upon the earth; and would that it were already kindled!" (Lk 12:49).

TUESDAY
WE CONSIDER ALL THINGS A LOSS TO GAIN CHRIST

But whatever gain I had, I counted as loss for the sake of Christ. Indeed I count everything as loss because of the surpassing worth of knowing Christ Jesus my Lord. For his sake I have suffered the loss of all things, and count them as refuse, in order that I may gain Christ and be found in him, not having a righteousness of my own, based on law, but that which is through faith in Christ, the righteousness from God that depends on faith; that I may know him and the power of his resurrection, and may share his sufferings, becoming like him in his death, that if possible I may attain the resurrection from the dead.

Philippians 3:7–11

The world values power, wealth, and position over faith. We are bombarded with the message that happiness comes from our possessions, our pleasures, and our accomplishments. Christians are not immune to the temptation to seek this sort of fulfillment. After all, can we not use our wealth and power for the cause of Christ? While it is true that we can, we must not allow our status and our stuff to become idols, or to base our worth on them. In the grand vision of eternity, they are insignificant. No matter how much good we do with them, they will vanish like smoke at the End of Days.

Only in our Savior do we obtain righteousness and overcome our sufferings to attain the peace and joy of the resurrection. This does not mean that we have to give up our earthly goods. It does mean that they cannot have a greater hold on us than our Lord does. Our possessions are really a gracious loan, given to us to be used for the kingdom. As we consider all things loss for the sake of knowing Jesus, we become conformed to his image and obtain the resurrection life given to us by God.

Questions for Reflection

What power, prestige, and possessions have you given up in order to find peace? What has that experience been like?

How can you share the resurrection life you have in Christ with another man today?

Praying with Scripture

"For whoever would save his life will lose it; and whoever loses his life for my sake and the gospel's will save it" (Mk 8:35).

WEDNESDAY
THERE ARE NO PARTICIPATION TROPHIES

Do you not know that in a race all the runners compete, but only one receives the prize? So run that you may obtain it. Every athlete exercises self-control in all things. They do it to receive a perishable wreath, but we an imperishable. Well, I do not run aimlessly, I do not box as one beating the air; but I pommel my body and subdue it, lest after preaching to others I myself should be disqualified.

1 Corinthians 9:24–27

It has been said that young people today have no idea what it means to win. A whole generation has grown up receiving praise and participation trophies for mediocre effort in sports, music, dance, and many other arenas. Instead of teaching our children to strive for the good and live disciplined lives for Christ, we too often settle for the easy message that everyone gets a trophy just for showing up. Granted, this refers to world-ly success alone. Still it has ramifications for the way we run the race for our souls.

God calls us to live out our Christian lives as a race to the finish line. We cannot be mere spectators of our faith. We need to jump in the game and give our all to the goal of getting to heaven. Too many Catholic men fail to get involved in the life of the Church, hoping instead that they can gain heaven from the bleachers. They stay away from the Mass and the sacraments, keep their Bibles closed, and make little time for prayer. God deserves better than that. The gospel is too important for us to keep to the sidelines of our faith. We need to be active partici-pants in sharing the Good News of Jesus with all the world.

Questions for Reflection
Do you participate actively in running the race to reach Christ?

What steps can you take to become more active in the Church?

What are the biggest obstacles in your life right now that might keep you from running and finishing the race?

Praying with Scripture
"I have fought the good fight, I have finished the race, I have kept the faith" (2 Tm 4:7).

THURSDAY
GOD STICKS BY THOSE WHO CARRY ON THE FIGHT

When you go forth to war against your enemies, and see horses and chariots and an army larger than your own, you shall not be afraid of them; for the LORD your God is with you, who brought you up out of the land of Egypt. And when you draw near to the battle, the priest shall come forward and speak to

*the people, and shall say to them, "Hear, O Israel, you draw
near this day to battle against your enemies: let not your heart
faint; do not fear, or tremble, or be in dread of them; for the
LORD your God is he that goes with you, to fight for you against
your enemies, to give you the victory."*

Deuteronomy 20:1–4

As men, we face many battles in our daily living. If Christ is
not the center of our lives, we will surrender to fear and ultimately fall short of victory. We are weak, but God is strong.
With his help we become winners who move forward against
the enemies that assail us. We fight with his power flowing
through us, knowing that it has no limit.

We need to put aside our impulse to fight with our own
strength, and accept that the Spirit of God will win the victory
in and through us. We must act, but in the end God gives the
victory. Yes, we may stumble along the way, make selfish decisions, and sometimes lose sight of the source of our strength.
But God calls us to surrender to his never-failing care, remembering we are servant soldiers following his lead as we wage the
war to overcome evil.

Questions for Reflection

What does real victory in Christ look like, and how has it manifested itself in your life?

How can you yield more fully to the reality that God will never
forsake you?

What specific battles in your life are you facing today? Where
do you need to ask for God's help?

Praying with Scripture

"Have I not commanded you? Be strong and of good courage;
be not frightened, neither be dismayed; for the LORD your God
is with you wherever you go" (Jos 1:9).

FRIDAY
Hope Turns Weaklings into Eagles

Have you not known? Have you not heard?
*The L*ORD *is the everlasting God,*
    the Creator of the ends of the earth.
He does not faint or grow weary,
    his understanding is unsearchable.
He gives power to the faint,
    and to him who has no might he increases strength.
Even youths shall faint and be weary,
    and young men shall fall exhausted;
*but they who wait for the L*ORD *shall renew their strength,*
    they shall mount up with wings like eagles,
they shall run and not be weary,
    they shall walk and not faint.

Isaiah 40:28–31

Although modern culture tries to portray men as pathetic and ineffectual losers who have little ambition and no sense of purpose, most men hate to be perceived as timid or unsuccessful. Because of society's perceptions of men, we often feel that if we just work harder and get tougher, we will accomplish all our goals in life. We can fall prey to the false notion that relying on God strips us of our identity. In truth, yielding to the Almighty transforms how we understand in the deepest sense what it means to be a man.

When we become new creations in Christ, hope transforms us from weaklings into soaring eagles. We move forward in faith, striving with his strength and living a renewed and meaningful existence. Who we are is fundamentally changed. We no longer perceive loss and gain in terms of worldly achievement or wealth. Rather, we seek our true victory, which comes from Christ. Remade in the image of Christ, we are ready to use our gifts in his service, relying on God as our strength and our source of victory.

Questions for Reflection

Do you see a difference between the man you are now and the man you were before you deepened your commitment to God? What are some of the key aspects of that difference?

Do you see yourself as a new man in Christ?

How has surrendering to Christ changed the way you view your life calling and your work?

Praying with Scripture

"The LORD is my strength and my song; / he has become my salvation" (Ps 118:14).

SATURDAY

Go Deeper

Where has God given me supernatural strength for living my everyday life this week? Have I thanked him and given him all the glory?

_____

_____

_____

_____

_____

Am I grateful for the gifts God has given me? Where have I failed to thank him?

_____

_____

_____

_____

_____

How have I responded to the division that faith brings to my life? Am I bitter and resentful? How can I surrender even that to the Lord in trust?

_____

_____

_____

_____

What have I given up for Christ? What have I gained from committing to him? Has it been worth it?

_____

_____

_____

_____

_____

Do I go "all-in" for the gospel, or am I content to sit on the sidelines? How can I become more engaged in my faith?

_____

_____

_____

_____

_____

Have I shared the grace I have received from being a new creation in Christ? How can I share even more generously going forward?

_____

_____

_____

_____

_____

WEEK 8

SINS OF THE FATHERS AND LOVING LEGACIES

And the LORD descended in the cloud and stood with him there, and proclaimed the name of the LORD. The LORD passed before him, and proclaimed, "The LORD, the LORD, a God merciful and gracious, slow to anger, and abounding in mercy and faithfulness, keeping merciful love for thousands, forgiving iniquity and transgression and sin, but who will by no means clear the guilty, visiting the iniquity of the fathers upon the children and the children's children, to the third and the fourth generation."

Exodus 34:5–7

As men, one of our biggest concerns is whether we will leave a lasting legacy upon this earth. We spend our lives learning, growing, achieving, and striving to be more, and we wonder if what we do really matters. As Catholic men, we also ask ourselves if we are living as God desires. Are we being the best husband, father, Christian brother, and Catholic man we can be? If we are honest with ourselves, we know that many times we fall short.

God's love has the power to turn our failures into lasting legacies. By his grace we can become the men we are meant to be. We can pass on his love and strength to others: our children, our Church, and our community. We cannot take this awesome responsibility lightly because, just as we pass on the good given to us in Christ, so too can we pass on sinful habits, bitterness and pain, and the inner resistance to God that we hold on to in our lives.

How can we pass on grace and glory, rather than guilt and godlessness? This week we will consider the following truths:

1. While sin can touch several generations, God's love extends into eternity.

Some focus so much on God's justice that they cannot move past the pain and sorrow from their past to become the men God calls them to be. This can be especially difficult for men who may have received a legacy of sin and pain from their own earthly fathers. But God's love can break into our lives and lead us to the path of love. His mercy can undo the damage of generational sin, freeing us to pass on a legacy of love to those who come after us.

2. God's mercy is tied to the slowness of his anger.

If God treated us as our sins deserved, we would not survive. But he is a loving Father who is eternally patient with his children, giving us time to repent and return to him. He has given us the Church and the sacraments to provide us with grace and to draw us back to him when we fall. Our patient God loves us enough to move at our pace and wait for us as we mature.

3. Ultimately God does not punish us for the sins of our fathers.

In the Old Testament, the law stated that children should not suffer for the sins of their parents, but only for their own sins (cf. Dt 24:16). The cycle of pain can give way to a heritage of grace, if we allow God to work in our lives. When we accept the mercy of God, we can find forgiveness and new life in Christ.

4. The Lord of the universe loved us enough to come down to meet us.

God chooses to enter our lives through the powerful love of Christ. No matter what our past might hold, God wants to be part of our journey and to transform us into men after his own heart. It is an awesome thing to stand before our God and let his great love overshadow us in order to transform us into saints.

5. Our legacy begins with love, continues with teaching, and ends with integration.

If we love God with all our hearts, it will spill out into our whole life, healing our past and setting the course for the future. As God's love transforms us, it becomes a part of who we are, integrated into our words and actions, shaping how we pass on that love to future generations through our teaching and our example.

This Week's Call to Action

Spend time this week considering the legacy you received from your parents, especially your father, and what kind of legacy you wish to leave for future generations. Then take concrete steps to implement that legacy. How can you receive the love of Christ and show it to your family, your Church, and your world? Take care to make every word and deed a true reflection of the love Jesus has shown you. Let all you say and do leave a lasting impact on everyone you encounter.

Our Catholic legacy should be an enduring one. As we love with the tender, obedient, and sacrificial love of Christ, we bear eternal fruit in the world. We can leave no better legacy to our children, our Church, and our world than to be living examples of that same love that led Jesus to bleed and die on the cross so we can have a lasting legacy in heaven.

SUNDAY

This week we will consider what it means to leave a lasting legacy for those who will come after us. Moreover, we will explore the great truth that we don't have to carry the burden of our fathers' sins. Thanks to God's merciful love, we can break free to live out God's eternal plan for our lives. We work out our salvation by turning these great truths into practical acts of love for others, trusting that those actions will help shape future generations of faithful believers.

This Sunday reflect on the Mass, which is all about the lasting, loving legacy of Christ. The Liturgy of the Word reminds us of the eternal story of God's love, which is acted out upon the stage of humanity. The prayers and blessings throughout the Mass draw us deeper into the relationship we share with Christ in the Eucharist. The fellowship we share with other believers is a beautiful picture of how the legacy of Christianity is passed down through the ages.

Questions for Reflection

Do you accept the mercy of God in your life? If not, what holds you back?

Do you love others the way Jesus has loved you, or do you treat people with little respect, dignity, or kindness?

What concrete steps are you taking in your life to pass on to future generations the power and presence of Christ?

Praying with Scripture

"So we know and believe the love God has for us. God is love, and he who abides in love abides in God, and God abides in him" (1 Jn 4:16).

MONDAY
WHILE SIN CAN TOUCH SEVERAL GENERATIONS, GOD'S LOVE EXTENDS INTO ETERNITY

*And you he made alive, when you were dead through the tres-
passes and sins in which you once walked, following the course
of this world, following the prince of the power of the air, the
spirit that is now at work in the sons of disobedience. Among
these we all once lived in the passions of our flesh, following the
desires of body and mind, and so we were by nature children of
wrath, like the rest of mankind. But God, who is rich in mercy,
out of the great love with which he loved us, even when we were
dead through our trespasses, made us alive together with Christ
(by grace you have been saved), and raised us up with him, and
made us sit with him in the heavenly places in Christ Jesus,
that in the coming ages he might show the immeasurable riches
of his grace in kindness toward us in Christ Jesus.*

Ephesians 2:1–7

Exodus 20:5 talks about God inflicting punishment on those
who hate him, to the third and fourth generation. Does this
mean each of us carries the responsibility for our fathers' sins
(and our grandfathers', great-grandfathers', etc.)? No. Our sinful life choices can have terrible consequences for our children
and their children for years to come, but God does not punish
anyone for the sins of his parents. No one is responsible for the
guilt of his fathers.

Moreover, God's love reaches much further than his justice. His mercy is eternal, powerful, and perfect. It extends into
the lives of even the most sinful among us and brings resto-
ration and new meaning, with consequences that impact generations far into the future.

The great love of God digs deeply into our broken hearts
and empowers us to overcome the consequences of any sin that
has been passed on to us that may cause us sorrow. In his mercy

we can experience new hope. As we walk the path of God's love, we can overcome the generational sin that has such a hold on our lives. Instead of allowing the consequences of the sins of our fathers to shape our identities or define our actions, we can begin a new and blessed chapter in our lives, forging a new path for those who come after us.

Questions for Reflection

Where have you experienced the consequences of generational sin in your life?

Have you seen God's great love break the hold of past sin and put you on a new path? What was the result?

How do you want to pass on God's love for you to the generations after you?

Praying with Scripture

"Beloved, we are God's children now; it does not yet appear what we shall be, but we know that when he appears we shall be like him, for we shall see him as he is" (1 Jn 3:2).

TUESDAY
God's Mercy Is Tied to the Slowness of His Anger

The LORD is merciful and gracious,
*   slow to anger and abounding in mercy.*
He will not always chide,
*   nor will he keep his anger for ever.*
He does not deal with us according to our sins,
*   nor repay us according to our iniquities.*

Psalm 103:8–10

Nearly every man has held, is holding, or will hold a grudge against another person at some point in his life. It is part of our fallen nature to want revenge for the wrongs done to us. God, however, is not like us and does not remain angry with his people. If he did, who could stand before him? He is a compassionate Father who is slow to anger, full of mercy, and perfectly loving. He remembers that we are fragile beings, formed out of the dust, a mist that appears for a little while and then vanishes (cf. Jas 4:14). Yet God chooses not to remember our sins; and when we repent, he hurls them as far from us as the east is from the west (cf. Ps 103:12).

God's incredible patience is intimately tied to his mercy. His is an eternal love, a timeless compassion that he pours out on us through his Son. As members of his Mystical Body, we have a deep and personal relationship with God that will never fade or overwhelm our brittle human nature. He stands at the door of our hearts, knocking and waiting with infinite patience for us to invite him in so he can change our lives and set us free to love and serve him and others (cf. Rv 3:20).

Questions for Reflection
Where have you experienced the perfect and infinite mercy of God in your life?

How do you see God's patient love displayed through the Church and the sacraments?

How can you take that perfect, merciful love and share it with someone else today?

Praying with Scripture
"The Lord is gracious and merciful, slow to anger and abounding in mercy" (Ps 145:8).

WEDNESDAY
ULTIMATELY GOD DOES NOT PUNISH US FOR THE SINS OF OUR FATHERS

The fathers shall not be put to death for the children, nor shall the children be put to death for the fathers; every man shall be put to death for his own sin.

Deuteronomy 24:16

The soul that sins shall die. The son shall not suffer for the iniquity of the father, nor the father suffer for the iniquity of the son; the righteousness of the righteous shall be upon himself, and the wickedness of the wicked shall be upon himself.

Ezekiel 18:20

Although the sins of a father often bring negative consequences to his descendants, God is merciful in administering justice. While he does not punish us for sins we have not committed, sadly, the consequences of sin are far-reaching, and God does permit them to fall even on the innocent. This is part of the mystery of evil and the even greater mystery of human freedom. Yet God works all things to the good for those who love him and place their trust in him. No matter what we may suffer due to our fathers' sins, God's goodness and mercy are infinitely more powerful.

The awesome truth is that we can break the cycle of pain through the power of God's grace. As we take hold of the great truth that God loves us with a perfect and all-powerful love, we become purposeful and powerful men of God, able to change our world through the good of the gospel. We are God's people, and he is our Lord.

Questions for Reflection
How have you been able to break from the sins of the past and live as a new creation? Where are you still seeking freedom?

How are you bringing the love you have found in Christ to the lost of this world?

Praying with Scripture
"Behold, all souls are mine; the soul of the father as well as the soul of the son is mine: the soul that sins shall die" (Ez 18:4).

THURSDAY
THE LORD OF THE UNIVERSE LOVED US ENOUGH TO COME DOWN TO MEET US

Since therefore the children share in flesh and blood, he himself likewise partook of the same nature, that through death he might destroy him who has the power of death, that is, the devil, and deliver all those who through fear of death were subject to lifelong bondage. For surely it is not with angels that he is concerned but with the descendants of Abraham. Therefore he had to be made like his brethren in every respect, so that he might become a merciful and faithful high priest in the service of God, to make expiation for the sins of the people. For because he himself has suffered and been tempted, he is able to help those who are tempted.

Hebrews 2:14–18

Many Christians have memorized John 3:16 ("For God so loved the world ... "). We see the verse displayed in sports stadiums and on T-shirts. We proclaim it proudly as the foundation of our faith. But do we really understand the significance of that event? God, in his perfect, precious love, sent his Son to be born as a human being, to walk the dusty roads of this world, to face the trials and tribulations of earthly living, and ultimately to take all of our sins to the cruel cross so we could be saved.

Let that sink in for a moment: the Lord of the universe, whose hand set the stars in place, came to be our brother to set us free from sin and draw us back to himself.

Before Christ came, God often manifested his powerful presence to his people in the form of a fiery cloud, in peals of thunder, in earthquakes, and in the awesome whisper of his majestic voice. But now in Jesus we have a brother. We can experience the very presence of Christ in the sacraments, particularly the Eucharist, and in the fellowship of the Church that has been guided by the Holy Spirit for more than 2,000 years.

Questions for Reflection
Do you recognize Jesus as your brother? How has this awesome truth shaped your life as a Catholic man?

How does Christ's brotherhood with you impact your fellowship with other men? How can you strive to be Christ to those who need him most?

Praying with Scripture
"For God so loved the world that he gave his only-begotten Son, that whoever believes in him should not perish but have eternal life" (Jn 3:16).

FRIDAY
OUR LEGACY BEGINS WITH LOVE, CONTINUES WITH TEACHING, AND ENDS WITH INTEGRATION

Hear, O Israel: The LORD our God is one LORD; and you shall love the LORD your God with all your heart, and with all your soul, and with all your might. And these words which I command you this day shall be upon your heart; and you shall teach them diligently to your children, and shall talk of them when you sit in your house, and when you walk by the way, and when you lie down, and when you rise. And you shall bind them as a sign upon your hand, and they shall be as frontlets

*between your eyes. And you shall write them on the doorposts
of your house and on your gates.*

Deuteronomy 6:4–9

This is the Shema, the legacy prayer of the Jewish people. It expresses the first and greatest commandment, reaffirmed by Christ in Mark's Gospel (cf. 12:30). If we desire to leave a lasting legacy of love upon the earth, we must begin with the love of the immutable, all-powerful, and ever-present Lord of the universe. If we truly allow that love to fill our lives, it will pour out from our hearts into the lives of those around us through our words and actions. It is of primary importance that we pass on to others the Law of Love we have received.

We must share that love through our every word and our every act of service. God's love should spill out into our homes as we establish all we do upon the rock that is Christ. In this way our legacy will be grounded in love, actualized by our words and deeds, and integrated into our lives in the glory it returns to God. This powerful love moves in us from first to last, faith to faith, leading us and future generations to the kingdom of heaven.

Questions for Reflection

How does God's love spill out from you into the lives of those around you?

Is love the foundation of your home? Where can you show more love to your family and those in your household?

In what specific ways are you passing on the legacy of God's love to future generations?

Praying with Scripture

"Train up a child in the way he should go, and when he is old he will not depart from it" (Prv 22:6).

SATURDAY

Go Deeper

Do I believe in the power of God's amazing love to transform my life and overcome my past? Where do I struggle to accept this reality?

_____

_____

_____

_____

Where has God been most patient and forgiving with me in my life? Have I thanked him?

_____

_____

_____

_____

What generational sins hold me back from living fully for God? Where is God inviting me to surrender these wounds to his healing touch?

_____

_____

_____

_____

_____

_____

Have I lived out my faith in acts of love for others? Where can I live out this love more generously at home, at work, and in my daily encounters?

_____

_____

_____

_____

_____

_____

What legacy am I leaving for future generations? Is it a legacy of the love I have received from Christ? Am I willing to ask God for the strength to pass on his truth?

_____

_____

_____

_____

WEEK 9

DANCE LIKE NO ONE IS WATCHING . . . BUT BE READY FOR A LITTLE RIDICULE

As the ark of the LORD came into the city of David, Michal the daughter of Saul looked out of the window, and saw King David leaping and dancing before the LORD; and she despised him in her heart. ... And David returned to bless his household. But Michal the daughter of Saul came out to meet David, and said, "How the king of Israel honored himself today, uncovering himself today before the eyes of his servants' maids, as one of the vulgar fellows shamelessly uncovers himself!" And David said to Michal, "It was before the LORD, who chose me above your father, and above all his house, to appoint me as prince over Israel, the people of the LORD — and I will make merry before the LORD. I will make myself yet more contemptible than this, and I will be abased in your eyes; but by the maids of whom you have spoken, by them I shall be held in honor."

2 Samuel 6:16, 20–22

Do we know how to celebrate our Catholic Faith with all our heart, mind, and soul? Do we respond to the mystery and majesty of our life in Christ with the same passion and enthusiasm we display for our hobbies or sports teams? Or has our Catholicism become routine? We shout at the top of our lungs when a superstar makes a winning score or sings our favorite song, yet we yawn our way through Sunday Mass, unmoved by the great mystery of the Eucharist unfolding before us. We hang on every word as a remodeling expert shows us how to tackle the latest home improvement project, but we barely remember the message of the latest homily. Something is very wrong with this picture.

Catholic men need to gain a new perspective on what it means to belong to Christ. We need to follow the example of King David, who danced like a madman before the Ark of the Lord. How can we begin to live a more unashamed love for our faith? This week we will consider five key realities that can help us with this:

1. God has given us his best, and we owe him our best.
Just as God gave his presence to the people of Israel, he gives us the presence of Christ in the Word and the Eucharist. Every celebration of the Mass should bring us great joy, and we should respond with our deepest love.

2. Our faith is not an exclusive club membership.
We often forget that salvation is a gift we have been given, not a privilege we deserve. Our chosen status should be a call to tell all the world of the greatness of God, who gave his Son for our sins.

3. What some dismiss and despise, we wear as a garment of praise.
Yes, the world may look at our enthusiasm for our faith as a kind of insanity, but that should not curb our passion or stifle us into submission. Instead we should hold our heads up high and press on with joy.

4. God's power and presence lead us to overflowing gratitude.
Psalm 100 is a perfect example of the thanksgiving that should flow from our lips. God's goodness to us leads us to joyful service, humble submission, thankful praise, and perfect rest.

5. Our thanksgiving should manifest itself in words and actions.

Not only should praise flow naturally from our lips in our prayers and our speech, but we should be moving through our days with the grace-filled joy of a holy dancer, knowing we are moving in step with our loving God.

This Week's Call to Action

There are few things as powerful as a man who is unashamed about his faith. This week determine to show others that you are blessed to be a Catholic man. Let every word and every action celebrate and shout to the world the joy you have as a man of faith. Meditate on your ever-deepening relationship with your Savior, who has graced you to live an abundant and immensely joyful existence as a member of his Mystical Body.

SUNDAY

This is all about giving God your best, knowing he has given you his best in Christ. Celebrate that God has chosen you to be his son and set you free because of his great love and mercy. Our only response to this love should be praise, as we loudly and proudly share who we are as Catholic men. God's overflowing presence in our lives should spill over in praise and in acts of love. This is how we share God's greatness with the world around us.

This Sunday pay careful attention to the readings at Mass. Look for how they express who God is and how he works in the lives of his people. As you listen to the words of the Eucharistic Prayer, lift up your own prayers of gratitude for the gift Christ has given you in his once-for-all sacrifice on the cross. As you receive the Eucharist, spend time with Jesus thanking him for all he has done for you throughout your life.

Questions for Reflection

Would you consider yourself a "loud and proud" worshipper? Why or why not?

How are you letting God's grace overflow into the lives of others through acts of love?

What are you most grateful for about your Catholic Faith?

Praying with Scripture

"Make a joyful noise to the LORD, all the earth; break forth into joyous song and sing praises" (Ps 98:4)!

MONDAY
GOD HAS GIVEN US HIS BEST, AND WE OWE HIM OUR BEST

The LORD is my chosen portion and my cup;
*   you hold my lot.*
The lines have fallen for me in pleasant places;
*   yes, I have a goodly heritage.*
I bless the LORD who gives me counsel;
*   in the night also my heart instructs me.*
I keep the LORD always before me;
*   because he is at my right hand, I shall not be moved.*

                                        Psalm 16:5–8

What an awesome privilege we have to belong to Jesus. We will never fully understand on this side of heaven what it means to be members of the Body of Christ, yet we know we have been given an inheritance in heaven for all eternity. We have the Holy Spirit, who counsels us and guides the Church into all truth. We have countless blessings of provision and strength as we live each day as disciples of the Lord. We experience joy and can rest secure, even when the circumstances of our lives bring suffering and sorrow. We are never abandoned, never forsaken, and forever called to stand in the presence of the Almighty. Truly God gives us his best.

We must respond to this precious promise of love by giving God our very best. This means making a deeper commitment to be men who are sold-out for our Catholic Faith. Does this mean we will be free from failure, doubt, or sorrow? Of course not. But it does mean that we will seek the wonderful hope and abundant blessings given to us in Christ. As we live out our faith, we can give God praise, thanksgiving, and dedicated service. God gives us his whole self. The least we can do is to give our entire lives back to him.

Questions for Reflection

Where have you seen God's abundant blessings revealed in your life?

What specifically can you do to give yourself more fully to the One who died for you?

What have been some of your greatest joys in being a member of the Church?

Praying with Scripture

"Do your best to present yourself to God as one approved, a workman who has no need to be ashamed, rightly handling the word of truth" (2 Tm 2:15).

TUESDAY
OUR FAITH IS NOT AN EXCLUSIVE CLUB MEMBERSHIP

In him, according to the purpose of him who accomplishes all things according to the counsel of his will, we who first hoped in

*Christ have been destined and appointed to live for the praise
of his glory. In him you also, who have heard the word of truth,
the gospel of your salvation, and have believed in him, were
sealed with the promised Holy Spirit, who is the guarantee of
our inheritance until we acquire possession of it, to the praise of
his glory.*

Ephesians 1:11–14

There is a temptation to treat our Catholic Faith like a membership in an elite, private club. While we certainly do share in the
abundant riches that come with membership in the Church,
we are far from privileged associates in an organization that
cannot live without us. God does not exist to meet our needs;
rather, we exist to reflect God's glory.

Every day we should be sharing our faith with gratitude
and joy that knows no bounds. We were sinners bound for hell,
undeserving of any privilege, unworthy of God's love, yet he
has given us salvation, sonship, and a secure place in his kingdom, where we are called to live for his praise and glory. That
knowledge should have us cheering in the streets, or at least sitting up and joyfully praising our Savior each Sunday at Mass.
If we have been given the first installment of a greater glory to
come, how can we fail to share that glory with the whole world?

Questions for Reflection

Do you recognize that your position in Christ is an underserved
gift? How are you tempted to view it as a privilege?

Where can you bring a greater attitude of thanksgiving into
your prayer?

How are you sharing with those around you the joy you have in
being a member of the Body of Christ?

Praying with Scripture

"He who brings thanksgiving as his sacrifice honors me; to

him who orders his way aright
I will show the salvation of God" (Ps 50:23)!

WEDNESDAY
WHAT SOME DISMISS AND DESPISE, WE WEAR AS A GARMENT OF PRAISE

Awake, awake,
>   *put on your strength, O Zion;*
put on your beautiful garments,
>   *O Jerusalem, the holy city;*
for there shall no more come into you
>   *the uncircumcised and the unclean.*
Shake yourself from the dust, arise,
>   *O captive Jerusalem;*
loose the bonds from your neck,
>   *O captive daughter of Zion.*
>   *For thus says the* LORD: *"You were sold for nothing, and*
you shall be redeemed without money."

Isaiah 52:1–3

Most of us will never know what it is like to live in captivity, though certainly there are those among us who have faced prison, divorce, addiction, loneliness, depression, and many other painful forms of spiritual bondage. Yet when we encounter Jesus and his redeeming love, we are able to shake off the dust of desolation, loose the bonds of oppression and fear, and rejoice with great gladness over our new life in Christ. We can proudly wear this garment of praise and proclaim the joy that is ours as Catholics.

The Bible compares our resurrection life to waking from a nightmarish slumber. In the light of Christ's love, we see clearly what it means to walk as a believer robed in our salvation. We have been set free from the tyranny of sin and the captivity of our fallen lives. Even if we continue to face struggles, we do so with the grace of our faith to sustain us through the hard times. That truth should lead to open, unceasing, and joyful praise!

Questions for Reflection

What forms of captivity have you experienced during your life? Are there any that you still experience?

How has Jesus rescued you from the nightmare of sin to revel in his strength?

Do you allow Jesus' resurrection life to lead you to joyful praise and Christlike action toward others? What impact has this had on you and on the people in your life?

Praying with Scripture

"Through him then let us continually offer up a sacrifice of praise to God, that is, the fruit of lips that acknowledge his name" (Heb 13:15).

THURSDAY
GOD'S POWER AND PRESENCE LEAD US TO A STATE OF OVERFLOWING GRATITUDE

Make a joyful noise to the LORD, all the lands!
    Serve the LORD with gladness!
    Come into his presence with singing!
Know that the LORD is God!
    It is he that made us, and we are his;
    we are his people, and the sheep of his pasture.
Enter his gates with thanksgiving,
    and his courts with praise!
    Give thanks to him, bless his name!
For the LORD is good;

his mercy endures for ever,
and his faithfulness to all generations.

Psalm 100

Psalm 100 is a powerful prayer of thanksgiving that lays out a number of reasons why God deserves our praise. God is our Creator, who made us out of nothing. We belong to him not as slaves, but as precious children. We are the flock he leads with love and perfect care, providing for us abundantly. He brings us to our refuge, a holy city that is ours by our adoption as his children. We enter his courts, confident that we will be judged with mercy and forgiveness. He is a good God, merciful, loving, and faithful to the promises he has made, both now and forevermore.

God's goodness should lead us into passionate, powerful, and perfect praise. Our adoration should reflect the wondrous love of God that is poured out into our lives. As Catholics, we share in the salvation achieved on the cross by Christ. We exist as a Church to live out the reality of that great gift by our works of charity. Our praise flows from the abundant blessings God has given us through his Son.

Questions for Reflection
What reasons do you have for giving God your song of praise? Do you praise him, or do you find yourself holding back?

In what areas of your life do you need to work on being more thankful?

How are you sharing your gratitude and the reasons for it with others?

Praying with Scripture
"For it is all for your sake, so that as grace extends to more and more people it may increase thanksgiving, to the glory of God" (2 Cor 4:15).

FRIDAY
OUR THANKSGIVING SHOULD MANIFEST ITSELF IN WORDS AND ACTIONS

And we exhort you, brethren, admonish the idle, encourage the fainthearted, help the weak, be patient with them all. See that none of you repays evil for evil, but always seek to do good to one another and to all. Rejoice always, pray constantly, give thanks in all circumstances; for this is the will of God in Christ Jesus for you.

1 Thessalonians 5:14–18

Our Catholic Faith should be a fiery dance of joy, a determined march onto the battlefield of life, a holy, disciplined race toward the goal of heaven. As we live out what it means to be believers, we discover the peace, the power, and the persevering faith the Holy Spirit gives as he moves in our lives and accomplishes the will of God through us. It is a wonderful thing to be a channel of God's grace to the world.

Every word of the above passage exhorts us to turn our praise into powerful action that builds up the Body of Christ and gives glory and honor to God. We must move in this world with the passion that comes from living a Spirit-filled life, hating evil and holding fast to the good. As we spread the blessings we have received, we purify our hearts and change the world. We help to prepare for the coming of the Lord by our spotless lives and our unending, faithful praise.

Questions for Reflection

How is our faith made more beautiful and complete through gratitude and works of love?

Why does God call us to give thanks in all circumstances?

What can you do to make the God of peace more fully known to those around you?

Praying with Scripture
"Thanks be to God for his inexpressible gift!" (2 Cor 9:15).

SATURDAY

Go Deeper

Do I give God my best in all I say and do? If not, where do I give him only half-hearted efforts?

_____

_____

_____

_____

Do I celebrate my status as God's chosen son? Where have I taken my position in Christ for granted?

_____

_____

_____

_____

Do I wear a garment of praise proudly, even in the face of ridicule? Where have I refused to express my gratitude for fear of being mocked or misunderstood?

_____

_____

_____

_____

_____

Am I growing in gratitude to Christ through my prayer life?

_____

_____

_____

_____

Am I serving God by serving the Church he loves so much? Where can I give more?

_____

_____

_____

_____

_____

WEEK 10

REAL STRENGTH FOR REAL MEN

The LORD is my strength and my shield;
in him my heart trusts;
so I am helped, and my heart exults,
and with my song I give thanks to him.

Psalm 28:7

Fear not, for I am with you,
be not dismayed, for I am your God;
I will strengthen you, I will help you,
I will uphold you with my victorious right hand.

Isaiah 41:10

Remember not the former things,
nor consider the things of old.
Behold, I am doing a new thing;
now it springs forth, do you not perceive it?
I will make a way in the wilderness and rivers in the desert.

Isaiah 43:18–19

Every man fails. We are fallen creatures, stained by sin and lost without a Savior. When we stumble on the road of life, we can either live with the mistakes and allow them to destroy us, or we can pick ourselves up and begin again. The road to recovery is never easy. When our strength is gone and the world seems against us, the path may be unclear. But there is a way we can go.

The 1986 sports film *Hoosiers* (Orion Pictures) tells the story of a man who failed and was given a second chance. Norman Dale (Gene Hackman) was a New York college basketball coach for the Ithaca Warriors who was fired for physically assaulting one of his players during a crucial game. A former colleague hired him as a high school basketball coach in Hickory, Indiana. He was treated as an outsider by the people of the town, who challenged his every decision and eventually tried to have him fired. But one courageous player, Jimmy Chitwood, saved Coach Dale's job by declaring in front of the entire town, "If he goes, I go!" The Huskers went on to win the 1954 state basketball championship. Coach Dale faced enormous obstacles to win the hearts of the people of the town and lead his team to the championship. He discovered how to make the words of 1 Maccabees 3:19 his own: "It is not on the size of the army that victory in battle depends, but strength comes from Heaven."

As the film *Hoosiers* demonstrates so well, our second chances find their true fulfillment in the strength of God alone. What can we learn about God's strength for weary men who have failed? This week we will consider these points:

1. Without God every man will fail.

All men, when they seek their own way, will stumble and fall. We need God's strength to help us accomplish his purposes for our lives. When we do things on our own, we accomplish nothing but failure — even if it looks like success in the eyes of the world.

2. God's ways are not our ways, and we can thank him for that.

The Bible tells us, "For my thoughts are not your thoughts, / neither are your ways my ways, says the LORD " (Is 55:8). So many men rage against the will of God and end up exhausted and defeated. When we surrender to the truth that God is in charge, we receive the power we need to accomplish great things in his name.

3. Hope is the fountain of youth.

Even strong young men will fail without God (cf. Is 40:30). But all men can find new spiritual vitality and renewed purpose by submitting to God in trust, knowing he will give us what we need. In his strength our drive and determination are reborn.

4. In God our second chance can be our number-one accomplishment.

No matter how late we turn to God, he can make something great of our life if we live for the Lord. The mistakes of the past can give way to spiritual soaring and great personal triumph.

5. Real strength and real manhood come from submitting to the greater good.

As we surrender to God's purposes, we become caught up in the flow of his plan, and together with our brothers in faith, we work to carry it out. That humility is the essence of true manhood.

This Week's Call to Action

No matter what mistakes we have made in the past, God's renewing strength is always ready to pour itself into our lives. This week take time to reflect on the incredible gift of grace given to you in your Baptism, strengthened through Confession and Eucharist, and lived out within the family of the Church. Refuse to believe Satan's lie that your failures are too many to forgive, the obstacles in your path are too big to overcome, or the future before you is too frightening to face. Hold on to the truth that "strength comes from heaven" and live for God's glory and our good. Catholic men who accept their limitations and draw on God's strength to renew them day after day can show the world that with God's help, we can accomplish all that he desires for our lives.

SUNDAY

All men, when we seek our own way, stumble and fall. God's ways are not our ways, and submitting to his plan is the key to finding spiritual renewal. The God of second chances can do amazing things with a life surrendered to him. No matter what we have done in the past, when we turn our lives over to him, God allows us to become a living sacrifice before the throne of heaven as we serve humanity for the glory of Christ.

The Mass is our weekly spiritual workout. It is the place where we build our strength by allowing Christ to pour himself into our lives. As you come to the table this week, meditate on the reality that Jesus offers you real food and drink in the Eucharist. It is true nourishment for the journey of life. This Sunday truly yield to the power and presence of the One who is all you need.

Questions for Reflection

What mistakes can you cast aside today so that you can place your hope in the Lord, seek his strength, and find renewal?

How can you begin to live for him in your witness to others?

Praying with Scripture

"Behold, God is my salvation; / I will trust, and will not be afraid; for the LORD GOD is my strength and my song, / and he has become my salvation" (Is 12:2).

MONDAY
WITHOUT GOD EVERY MAN WILL FAIL

Do not love the world or the things in the world. If any one loves the world, love for the Father is not in him. For all that is in the world, the lust of the flesh and the lust of the eyes and the pride of life, is not of the Father but is of the world. And the world passes away, and the lust of it; but he who does the will of God abides for ever.

1 John 2:15–17

Love for the world is really hatred of God (cf. Jas 4:4). When we seek our own way and look for our joy in the temporary trappings of this life, there is only one end in store for us: eternal punishment in hell. We cannot be good enough, perform enough works, or pay a great enough price to buy our way into the kingdom. Only the grace of God, given to us through the cross, can accomplish what all the wealth and prestige in the world cannot.

We can receive the blessings God has in store for us only if we accept this truth. Rather than storing up earthly treasures that will pass away, we need to seek the grace of God to accomplish his will and live out the purpose for which he created us. Are we willing to forgo the fleeting pleasures of a worthless life spent in personal pursuits in order become God's adopted sons? Will we carry out the plans for us that were set in motion from eternity?

This is a life-or-death choice. If we rely with our own strength, we will all fail. Only in Christ can we become saints who succeed for the kingdom.

Questions for Reflection

How has your love for the world kept you from becoming the man God wants you to be? What can you surrender to him now?

What earthly treasures have you surrendered to God in order to take hold of his will? What impact has that had on your life?

In what specific areas do you see yourself making progress for the kingdom of God?

Praying with Scripture
"For the wages of sin is death, but the free gift of God is eternal life in Christ Jesus our Lord" (Rom 6:23).

TUESDAY
GOD'S WAYS ARE NOT OUR WAYS, AND WE CAN THANK HIM FOR THAT

The unspiritual man does not receive the gifts of the Spirit of God, for they are folly to him, and he is not able to understand them because they are spiritually discerned. The spiritual man judges all things, but is himself to be judged by no one. "For who has known the mind of the Lord so as to instruct him?" But we have the mind of Christ.

1 Corinthians 2:14–16

How many times do we seek to accomplish our human goals with our own strength, only to end up defeated in the end? Do we blame God for our failure instead of looking to our own ignorance and arrogance as the cause? There is only one way to live free from fear and worry, full of joy and determination, and fully united to the perfect will of God: we must put on the mind of Christ.

If more Catholic men were willing to surrender to the truth that God's ways are not ours, we would see greater spiritual renewal within the Church. We rage against what we perceive as God's lack of concern for our needs, and we fail to see the many blessings he showers upon us. Often the things we complain about the most are God's greatest blessings in disguise — if only we had eyes to see! If we would only practice gratitude more freely, we would experience greater openness in our lives and see daily miracles of grace unfolding through our works. Today let us stand in awe before the mysterious ways of our Almighty Father and thank him for his perfect, gentle love.

Questions for Reflection

Where are you trying to get God to do things your way?

Are you willing to ask him to change your thinking?

How can you become more surrendered to God's plan for your life?

What is one hidden blessing you can thank God for right now?

Praying with Scripture

"For my thoughts are not your thoughts, / neither are your ways my ways, says the LORD" (Is 55:8).

WEDNESDAY
HOPE IS THE FOUNTAIN OF YOUTH

The steadfast love of the LORD never ceases,
*   his mercies never come to an end;*
they are new every morning;
*   great is your faithfulness.*
"The LORD is my portion," says my soul,
*   "therefore I will hope in him."*
The LORD is good to those who wait for him,
*   to the soul that seeks him.*
It is good that one should wait quietly
*   for the salvation of the Lord.*

Lamentations 3:22–26

It can be easy to think of eternity as endless time rather than perfect timelessness. While we may not admit it, we sometimes wonder if God's patience ever wears thin, if his love is limited, or if his desire to care for us waxes and wanes. We use our frail lives as a frame of reference when considering the mind of the

Almighty. In truth God's concern and compassion are never exhausted. We experience them anew every morning. This is what hope is all about: taking hold of the beautiful evidence of God's mercy in our lives and letting it drive us forward into eternity.

When we allow God to be our portion and our hope, we connect with his eternal, timeless, patient love. We can rest in contentment and silent surrender to whatever God has in store for our lives. No matter what each day holds, when we fix our eyes on the hope we have in Christ, everything in our lives becomes new. We become strong, determined, joyful stewards of the eternal work of God manifesting itself in the life of the Body of Christ.

Questions for Reflection

Do you ever fear that God's mercy has a limit? What do you think causes this fear?

How can you become more mindful of the ways in which God's mercies are made new each morning?

How can you carry these ever new gifts of mercy into your everyday world?

Praying with Scripture

"So we do not lose heart. Though our outer man is wasting away, our inner man is being renewed every day" (2 Cor 4:16).

THURSDAY
IN GOD OUR SECOND CHANCE CAN BE OUR NUMBER-ONE ACCOMPLISHMENT

I called to the LORD, out of my distress,
*   and he answered me;*
out of the belly of Sheol I cried,

and you heard my voice.
For you cast me into the deep,
 into the heart of the seas,
 and the flood was round about me;
all your waves and your billows
 passed over me.
The waters closed in over me,
 the deep was round about me;
weeds were wrapped about my head
 at the roots of the mountains.
I went down to the land
 whose bars closed upon me for ever;
yet you brought up my life from the Pit,
 O LORD my God.

Jonah 2:2–6

Perhaps the most remarkable part of Jonah's prayer is that he prayed it from inside the belly of the fish. Even though he did not know what would happen to him, Jonah trusted that God would redeem him from his great sin. He remembered that God rescues his servants and sets their feet on a new path. From the watery grave of a fish's belly, Jonah was reborn to a new life of preaching to the lost people of Nineveh.

Jonah points us to the sacrifice of Jesus on the cross. Jesus even compared Jonah's three days in the belly of the great fish to the three days he would spend in the heart of the earth (cf. Mt 12:40). Jesus endured the darkness of the grave in order to be raised up on the third day to bring the word of salvation to all the lost. These verses tell us that God is in the business of giving his children second (and third and fourth) chances. His grace allows us to make our second chances a new and glorious beginning, where our sins are forgotten and we learn to put the kingdom first. When Jesus gives us new life, we go forth to share the gospel with all who are in need of salvation.

Questions for Reflection
Where has God given you a second chance in life? How are you using that second chance for his glory?

Why is it easier to see your need for God when you are in the lowest place?

How are you living out your second chance by your acts of love toward others?

Praying with Scripture
"I will extol you, O Lord, for you have drawn me up, and have not let my foes rejoice over me" (Ps 30:1).

FRIDAY
REAL STRENGTH AND REAL MANHOOD COME FROM SUBMITTING TO THE GREATER GOOD

For I through the law died to the law, that I might live to God. I have been crucified with Christ; it is no longer I who live, but Christ who lives in me; and the life I now live in the flesh I live by faith in the Son of God, who loved me and gave himself for me.
Galatians 2:19–20

I appeal to you therefore, brethren, by the mercies of God, to present your bodies as a living sacrifice, holy and acceptable to God, which is your spiritual worship.
Romans 12:1

It is a theme you surely recognize now as we come to the close of this study: surrendering ourselves to God, giving up all that we are in order to allow God to transform our lives. The old law must give way to the power of the cross. Death must yield to resurrection. The old man must die so that the new man can shake off the past and live in service to Christ. As we let go of the attractions and distractions of this world and embrace the grace that is ours in Christ, we become living sacrifices, poured out upon the altar of this world so that we can bring the power of the gospel to all we meet.

The more we take hold of the promises and the purposes of God, the more the Church will conform to the image of Christ. It is our task to help prepare the Bride for the Bridegroom. As we live as Catholic men, working side by side with our brothers in the Faith and building the kingdom of God one faithful step at a time, we become real and authentic men of God. It is in humility and service to others in the name of Christ that the essence of true manhood can be found.

Questions for Reflection
Why is surrender to God's mercy and God's plans so important to our lives as Catholic men?

In what areas of your life can you say that you have truly died to yourself and risen to Christ?

How does humility help us to carry the gospel to a weary world?

Praying with Scripture
"Humble yourselves therefore under the mighty hand of God, that in due time he may exalt you" (1 Pt 5:6).

SATURDAY

Go Deeper

What second chances have I received from God, and how am I living them out?

_____

_____

_____

_____

_____

How has Christ granted me a youthful renewal in his love and mercy? Have I thanked him?

_____

_____

_____

Have I sought God's strength to help overcome my failure and fear? In what ways am I still relying on my own strength?

_____

_____

_____

Have I yielded to the higher ways of God this week? If not, where can I work on surrendering?

_____

_____

_____

_____

_____

How have I turned my surrender to God into service for his Church? Where can I give with greater generosity?

_____

_____

_____

_____

What are my goals for the days and years ahead as I conclude this study? In particular, how can I remain connected with my brothers?

_____

_____

_____

Conclusion

We cannot call ourselves men of character unless we are willing to put our faith into action. Saint Francis is said to have taught that we should preach the gospel always, and use words only if necessary. Yes, sharing the gospel of Jesus involves speaking the great truths of our faith. But how will others believe those truths if we ourselves are not living them out by our actions? The journey of our Catholic Faith requires that the rubber meets the road from one experience of grace to another.

Being a man of action is part of what it means to witness to our wonderful faith in a broken world. May you continue to grow in your character and strive to serve the kingdom through acts of love motivated by the sacrifice of our Savior on the cross. You are an important part of the Church. God bless you for all you do and all you will do to be the Church in a world so desperate for what only Jesus Christ can give!

Acknowledgments

Mary Beth Baker, you took on this project with incredible skill, insight, and grace and helped to turn it into what it is today. Thank you for being bold enough to nudge me in new directions, for showing incredible patience, and most of all for treating my book as if it were the only one you were editing. You brought balance and focus to my vision. Our Sunday Visitor has been blessed by your dedication and love for the Lord.

Laura Wolfskill, you deserve a medal for poring over my manuscript looking for repeated Bible verses and strange turns of phrase. Thank you and your team for making me look good and for all the many little details you handled to make this project a success. You are my hero!

Jaymie Wolfe, thank you for seeing the potential in a manuscript that grew from a simple devotional into a God-honoring and beautiful Bible study. You took the seed and planted it, and now the harvest has come!

Our Sunday Visitor, bless you for all those Sunday School lessons I loved as a boy and used as a children's minister. It is an honor to have been brought into the family to share with others what those lessons have produced in me.

Ken Santopietro, who invited me to serve on the planning committee of the Connecticut Catholic Men's Conference — you are a true example of a selfless and caring Catholic man.

My little online musings for the conference became this book, and your support helped to carry me through.

My wife, Christina, and my three children, Adam Mark, Lina Rose, and Hope Elizabeth, you have continued to love a husband and father who is forever a work in progress. You are my joy, my strength, and my constant comfort. Thank you for your love and support through all the years.

Ines Davino, my wonderful mother-in-law, you gave me that first copy of the magazine that helped to revive my writing career. You never stopped believing in me and supporting my gift for words. Though I dedicated this work to your husband, I know his character has been shaped by the love and support that you have always shown him.

ABOUT THE AUTHOR

MARK C. MCCANN is an author and ministry consultant with over thirty years of ministry experience with children, youth, and families on the parish and diocesan levels. He has also worked as a host and producer on Christian radio and written for a number of Catholic magazines and websites, including *St. Anthony Messenger, Emmanuel Magazine,* and *Catholic Stand.* He lives in Connecticut with his wife and three children. Each day he follows his call to be a man of words. You can learn about Mark's writing and ministry by going to www.wordsnvisions.com.